Luc aricy SJ

Medjugorje Unfolds

Mary speaks to the world

Fowler Wright Books Ltd
The Mercier Press Ltd

Fowler Wright Books Limited
Burgess Street
Leominster
Herefordshire
England

The Mercier Press Limited
4 Bridge Street
Cork
Ireland

First Edition 1985
Reprinted 1987
Cover design by
Eddie McManus

Typeset by
Leominster Print

Printed by Litho Press Co., Midleton, Co. Cork.

The cover illustration
is from a cartoon by Harry Clarke
for the Annunciation Window, St Joseph's, Terenure, Dublin
and is used by permission.

ISBN 0 85244 039 1 (Fowler Wright)
ISBN 0 85342 757 1 (Mercier Press)

Contents

1. Our Lady of Peace

We have written this book not only as a report on what has happened at Medjugorje up to the present time, but also as a reflection in faith on the events at Medjugorje. We have tried to show the significance of those events for all of us.

We both believe firmly in the authenticity and the importance of the apparitions of the blessed Virgin Mary at Medjugorje. At the same time, as Catholics, we accept the future judgement of the Church. Cardinal Ratzinger in his book *Rapporto sulla Fede,* speaking of Medjugorje writes: "In this field, above all, patience is a fundamental element of the policy of our Congregation (Congregation for the Doctrine of the Faith). No apparition is indispensable to the faith; Revelation ceased with Jesus Christ. He only is Revelation. But this does not stop God from speaking to our times through simple people and also through extraordinary signs which denounce the shortcomings of the culture which dominates us, marked by rationalism and positivism. The apparitions of which the Church has officially approved - Lourdes and Fatima among others - have their place precisely in the development of the life of the Church in the last century. They show among other things that Revelation - being one, concluded and not to be superseded - is not dead, but alive and vital. For the rest - such as Medjugorje, about which I am not expressing any judgement, the case being still under examination by the Congregation - one of the signs of our times is that Marian 'apparitions' are being multiplied in the world. From Africa, for example, and from other continents, our appropriate section is gathering reports.

"One of our criteria is to separate the aspect of truth or presumed 'supernaturality' of the apparition from that of its spiritual fruit. The pilgrimages of ancient christianity were to places about which our modern critical spirit would be perplexed regarding the 'scientific truth' of their traditions. But this does not detract from the fact that these pilgrimages were fruitful, beneficial, important for the life of the Christian people. The problem is not so much modern hypercriticism (which culminates in, among other things, a new form of credulity), but in the vitality and the orthodoxy of the spiritual life which develops from these places." (*Rapporto sulla Fede* pg. 112, Edizione Paolini, Torino 1985. Our translation.)

The Cardinal's words express our sentiments in writing this book. The apparitions of the Mother of God at Fatima were not declared 'worthy of belief' until 1930, thirteen years after their occurrence. We may have to wait that long or longer for the Church to speak officially about Medjugorje. So, in the light of the fact that, like us, hundreds of thousands of Catholics and others accept that the Medjugorje apparitions are true, and that official Church approval is surely a long way off, we speak of the apparitions as factual, to avoid continually referring to them as 'alleged' or 'reported'.

Meanwhile, if the blessed Virgin Mary really is appearing, who could take the responsibility for suppressing her message? Moreover, the message coming from Medjugorje is the traditional teaching of the Church.

The story of Medjugorje is by now widely known - how on the evening of 24 June 1981, our Lady appeared on a stony hillside near one of the five villages of the parish of St James, Medjugorje, Yugoslavia. She was seen first by Ivanka Ivankovic, then fifteen years of age, and Mirjana Dragicevic, sixteen. They were joined by Vicka Ivankovic and Ivan Dragicevic, both aged sixteen. The following evening, Marija Pavlovic, sixteen, and Jakov Colò, ten, were added to the group.

These four girls and two boys have seen the blessed Virgin each evening since then, except that Mirjana's visions ceased on Christmas Day 1982, and those of Ivanka on 7 May 1985. Two other young people of the parish have received interior words and visions since December 1982. They are Jelena Vasilij and Marijana Vasilij, both ten years old at that time.

The blessed Virgin has asked that we call her "Queen of Peace"; she has said that she has come to reconcile all people. Peace, she has told the young people who see her, will come only from conversion. The way of conversion is four-fold: faith daily prayer, monthly confession, and fasting.

Early in 1985, Robert Faricy went to Medjugorje for a week to pray. Here is a short account of his trip. It serves as an introduction to the following chapters.

The trip to Medjugorje.

Jugoslavian Airlines flight 401 takes me from Rome to Split, a city of 150,000 people on the Adriatic coast of the republic of Croatia, one of the five semi-autonomous political and ethnic regions that make up the nation of Yugoslavia. I arrive in the evening; I must spend the night in a hotel, since the next bus for Medjugorje leaves at eight o'clock the next morning.

I find my hotel in the main square of the "old city," a large block of light-coloured stone pavement, tightly packed buildings, and narrow-arched streetways - once the palace of the Emperor Diocletian. I feel I am walking on and in history. No cars or buses; I could be in the fourth century.

Outside the old city, down by the bus and train stations near the waterfront, many people, especially young men, walk aimlessly or mill around. I count five groups of young men singing - two in bars, three in the street. The songs all sound the same: completely tuneless, with a medium-slow rhythm, mechanically sung.

The people on this Sunday night give me the impression of lacking élan, hope, purpose. Pleasant up to a point, courteous for the most part, they expect nothing, and they give nothing. Simple people, but outside the standard Mediterranean stereotype; they are quite unlike, say, the Italians or the Spaniards or the Greeks. They lack any Mediterranean flair. They dress not so much poorly as badly; they do not have a certain suavity, what we used to call "cool." The women's hair looks unstyled; one wonders where the hairdressers of Split are trained. Even the mannequins in the store windows dress in poor taste and are ugly, nearly grotesque. Croatian charm does not lie in appearances. Rather in this: that they try hard to please, with a carefree incompetence. They are likable.

Split, then, is a dull city, neither peaceful not frenetic - just restless, aimless, colorless. Like the songs sung this evening, Split is tuneless, with a medium-slow pace that does not go anywhere definite. Split's mediaeval past is now and forever. Nothing changes. No future, and so no hope. It is a quiet city. But not a peaceful one.

Less than twenty percent of the Split population are practising Catholics. Outside the cities, in the country, regular religious practice can go as high as ninety-five percent. But here in Split, communism has succeeded in reducing the importance and the practice of Catholicism. My destination, the village parish of Medjugorje, will be different.

Medjugorje today.

I've been to Medjugorje three times before this. The first time, in the fall of 1981, I had heard of the apparitions of our Lady, and I went by train from Rome to Split. There, I went to the archbishop's residence. Archbishop Frane Franic, a well-known theologian and an important figure of the Second Vatican Council, received me graciously, and sent me to Medjugorje in his car with a priest driver.

My second visit to Medjugorje resulted in a book, with Lucy Rooney, S.N.D., *Our Lady Queen of Peace: Medjugorje* (New York, Dublin, Leominster, 1984). The third time, I went just to pray there for a few days. And I smuggled out a manuscript by Svetozar Kraljevic, later published as *The Apparitions of Our Lady at Medjugorje* (Chicago, 1984).

This time I carry no religious books or manuscripts either into or out of Yugoslavia. A Texan friend had previously tried to take Father Kraljevic's book manuscript to the U.S., was arrested by local police, and spent two awful days in a rural jail in Herzegovina. On 29 December 1984, Father René Laurentin, the distinguished French theologian and expert on Marian apparitions, carried a few religious books on his way to Medjugorje; he was arrested, stripped naked, insulted, tried before a judge, fined heavily, given twelve hours to get out of the country, and forbidden to re-enter for a year.

Since I look neither prosperous nor important, the police never stop me. But I am careful just the same. Although a priest, I am wearing a necktie instead of a Roman collar, and I travel light. My confidence in my disguise is shattered, however, when the ticket-collector on the morning bus out of Split smiles at me and asks, "Medjugorje?" I admit it.

After a long ride along the Adriatic, and then inland along narrow winding roads through the rocks and brush of the harsh hills of Croatia and Herzegovina, at ten minutes to twelve I see Saint James' Church, the parish church of Medjugorje, far off on my right. Five minutes later, the ticket-collector motions me to get off the bus. I do, and follow a sign that reads, "Medjugorje." A twenty-minute walk brings me to the church.

Walking, I notice all the new homes that have been built and that are being built. Some of these, and some of the older houses, have signs now: "sobe, zimmer, rooms, chambre." The government, then, has granted a lot of building permits, and permission to take boarders. But, when I come to the church area, I see that the local communists have not relented in harassing the Franciscan sisters and priests. The sisters' convent burned down some years ago, but the local authorities will not grant any building permit for a new one. So four sisters and four priests have to share a small rectory built for one or two priests.

For that matter, the parish cannot obtain permission to build toilet facilities for the large number of pilgrims that come every day. Toilets are three holes in the ground, two for women and one for men. This makes matters especially difficult in the cold winters. I had thought of giving this chapter the title, "The Yugoslavian Government Won't Let Catholics Go to the Toilet" - as a kind of cry of outrage.

I have not telephoned ahead to tell the Franciscans of my arrival. Although other telephones in the area work quite well, the authorities have seen to it that the parish house telephone rarely functions. Telephoning from other countries is literally impossible; the calls are invariably blocked, sometimes by a pleasant chime. The Franciscans are surprised but happy to see me. And I am delighted to see them.

At five in the afternoon, we go to the church for the rosary. The church is already filling up. Hundreds of people join in saying the joyful and the sorrowful mysteries. We finish just before six, when the Mass begins. Tonight, Father Joseph Zovko is the principal celebrant. Father Zovko was the parish priest when the apparitions first began. The Yugoslavian government tried him for sedition and sentenced him to three and one half years of hard labor. After a year and a half of abuse, with no bible and no breviary, forbidden to say Mass, he was freed. Vatican pressure obtained his release on condition that he would never again be assigned to Medjugorje. The local people say he went to prison because he refused to lock the young people out of his church in the evenings; evenings are when the apparitions take place.

In fact, Mary appears and speaks to a group of young men and women every night about 5.45 in a small chapel just off the main altar. They wait for her there, reciting the rosary, sometimes alone and sometimes with one of the Franciscans. Promptly at 5.45 they kneel facing a small altar-table and begin to pray aloud, saying "Our Father"s, "Hail Mary"s and "Glory be"s until, after they've prayed a short while, our Lady appears. They say she looks like a young Croatian woman of that region: blue eyes, black hair, pink cheeks. She wears a long silver robe and a white veil; she stands, suspended in air, on a small grey cloud. They can see, hear, and touch her. The apparitions last only a few minutes. Then the young people open the door of the chapel to hear the Mass.

Father Zovko preaches quite a long homily. No one

stirs; no foot-shuffling or coughing. Almost everyone goes to Holy Communion. After Mass, one of the priests of the parish prays over the people for healing, standing at the altar with arms extended, and praying aloud at some length. Then we say together the glorious mysteries of the rosary and the litany of our Lady. The whole program takes three hours. Most of the people in the parish and many from the surrounding region do this every day.

Peace

What is it like at Medjugorje? Peaceful. Peaceful, even though under severe attack. The local bishop, highly emotional and impulsive, strongly opposes the five young people, the Franciscan priests and sisters, and the authenticity of the apparitions. Joining him is the whole Yugoslavian communist government structure, and especially the local country police force.

Many theologians, including Hans Urs von Balthasar, René Laurentin and Tomaso Beck, have spoken out in favour of the truth of the events at Medjugorje. So have Archbishop Frane Franic of Split and many other churchmen. The Pope is said to be quite favourable to Medjugorje. But they are not there. The local bishop and the communist police are.

And yet, around the church and up on the hill where Mary first appeared, peace is in the air. I can feel it. It seeps in through the many layers of clothing I wear against the bitter cold, seeps into my heart. I learn at Medjugorje that peace is a gift, not earned or won or even built, but given as God's grace.

Peace comes to us from God through Mary, the mediatrix of all grace. It comes into our hearts as his gift. It comes to me here, at Medjugorje, now.

Peace, then, is not merely the absence of violence, not is it simply good order and no disturbances. Peace is a positive quality. First of the heart, and then - when many hearts have it - of society. It is a grace, given in response to prayer and fasting to those who turn to God in conversion.

Peace cannot exist without hope, and - especially -

without hope in some kind of ultimate destiny. Thus, peace cannot exist without religion. When religious belief is missing, then our deepest aspirations - for God - are blocked, and we are inevitably restless. When our hearts are led to reach out to God, then there is partial fulfillment now of those longings, and the hope of ultimate fulfillment. And there comes peace. "You have made us for yourself, O Lord, and our hearts shall find no rest until they rest in you."

The chapters that follow center on a visit we made to Medjugorje in April 1985. Fathers Rafael Luevano and Helmut Leonard came with us to help us to study the various communities taking shape at Medjugorje. And we interviewed Ivanka, Vicka, Marija, Jakov, and Ivan, asking them particularly about their own spiritual lives.

In the second chapter, Sister Lucy describes our visit, including the interviews with Ivanka and Ivan. The interviews with Vicka, Marija, and Jakov were recorded, and they make up the third chapter. In Chapter Four, we describe the different communities in the parish. Chapter Five treats chiefly the opposition of the Bishop of Mostar to the apparitions, and the controversy and suffering that it has caused; it also takes up the attitudes of the other Yugoslavian bishops and of the Vatican. We describe and reflect on the content of the message of our Lady in Chapters Six and Seven, and on the form and often apocalyptic context of that message in Chapter Eight. The last chapter explains the prayers most recommended by our Lady at Medjugorje, besides the Mass: the rosary, the Stations of the Cross, the "Jesus rosary," and some prayers our Lady has dictated.

2. A Visit to Medjugorje

On a Friday afternoon in early spring, Father Bob Faricy, Father Rafael Luevano and I, Sister Lucy, left Rome for Yugoslavia. An hour later, at the Dubrovnik airport, Father Bob began negotiating a reasonable price for a taxi. But at that moment, a coach party of American tourists en route to Sarajevo offered to take us as far as Citluk. No sooner were we settled in the coach than its driver came to say that the taxi manager was threatening to sue the coach firm if they took us. We left the coach to interview the taxi manager who tried to explain/excuse, while our prospective taxi driver stood by, silently and obviously fearfully. It had to be the taxi or nothing - so we agreed on a reduced price and set off. As we loaded our bags, a policeman asked the driver our destination, but made no attempt to stop us.

The drive is beautiful; first along the Adriatic coast at sunset, then inland through the mountains, always following the broad river Neretva. Our young driver Niko was no communist. He showed us the crucifix he always carries, and said the rosary with us.

It was dark when we arrived at the Medjugorje turn-off, and, unusually, there were no police and so no search of our bags. The crowds were just leaving the church after evening Mass, so we met the Franciscan community, priests and sisters. All were as welcoming as ever, and, typical of their kindness in the midst of hectic lives, they arranged for us to be driven up to the house where we would stay. Father Dobroslav drove, and Sister Janja came with us to see us well settled with Jozo. I had stayed before with Jozo, his mother Anda, his wife Marica and their four lovely blonde children: Ivana, nine, speaking a little English; Mate, seven, engrossed in his own affairs; Angelina, five, shy and charming; and Marija, two, who wrinkled her little nose with pleasure every time we met in the following days.

Saturday. The first day and the nights were bitterly cold because Medjugorje is ringed by mountains, snow-covered still. But each day was appreciably warmer and we watched the snow recede. Our house was at the foot of Mount Krizevac, the hill of the cross. It is 540 meters high with a winding rocky path to the cross on the crest. Father Bob was up there before dawn, making the Stations of the Cross with Sister Ignatia despite their having not one word of language in common!

Father Bob and I met that morning with Father Svetozar Kraljevic who was over from his parish at Ljubuski. Father Svet worked for two years in New York, but on a visit home to Yugoslavia was deprived of his passport and so has been unable to leave the country since. Like the priests in the parish, he is about forty years old and a member of the Croatian Province of the Friars Minor, or Franciscans; he has a gentle and mild manner that goes well with his fair and slender appearance. His sincerity and humility make themselves evident; you trust him almost on sight. Father Svet comes to the parish often, and has charge of all press relations, the translations into English of the messages and of accounts of the facts. His was the manuscript which Father Bob smuggled out, and which I once carried back in again. He told us of the most recent messages of our Lady to the parish.

Later there was a Mass in English for a group from the United States. Father Svet told the pilgrims that they probably would not see the five visionaries, nor probably would they see signs and wonders, but if they had open hearts they would receive at Medjugorje graces beyond their expectations. He added: "There are people in the parish who have grown spiritually even more than the visionaries. They are those who have accepted this Christian way of life (taught by our Lady) and have dared to start on it." Unfortunately the impact of his words was lessened by a priest who spoke after him, who was concerned with seeing the sun spin and other things peripheral.

The community invited Father Bob and me to dinner, and there we met the four Sisters: Janja, Ignatia, Melania and Amalia, and Fathers Tomislav Pervan, Dobroslav,

Slavko and Pero. Sisters Janja Boros and Melania are the closest to the young people to whom our Lady comes daily. One or both of these Franciscan sisters stays with them during the apparitions, praying with them before and after our Lady's visits. Sister Janja, attractive and outgoing, speaks excellent New York English. Besides seeing to the cooking of all the meals for the four Franciscan priests and the four sisters and, frequently, visiting Franciscans, Sister Janja helps English-speaking pilgrims in any way she can. And, like Sister Melania, she stays close to the five "visionaries" at Medjugorje: Vicka, Ivan, Ivanka, Marija, Jakov. Sister Melania, in her twenties, radiant and beautiful with blonde hair under her veil, and bright blue eyes, smiles a lot, works around the parish cleaning, doing laundry, helping in the kitchen and in the bookstore, speaking with pilgrims. Sister Ignatia and Sister Amalia, older and quieter, do the same kind of work. Sister Ignatia is the church sacristan, and she frequently prays with Jelena Vasilj and Marijana Vasilj, the two young girls who see and speak with our Lady frequently - sometimes in Sister Ignatia's room, while praying with her - although they are not a part of the regular small group that our Lady visits every evening.

Father Tomislav Pervan is the pastor of Saint James' parish, the parish at Medjugorje. He is a well-qualified biblical scholar, deliverate and kind in everything he does. Father Slavko Barbaric acts as spiritual guide for Vicka, Ivan, Ivanka, Marija, and Jakov; and also for Jelena and Marijana. A brilliant mind and driving energy help him to do a prodigious amount of work. His doctoral thesis on the subject of conversion prepared him for the work he does now: spiritual direction of young people who receive great graces, preaching in several languages (Croatian, German, French, Italian), guiding and counselling pilgrims. Fathers Pero and Dobroslav, besides the regular pastoral work in any large active parish, minister to the increasing number of pilgrims who come to Medjugorje seeking the Lord because they have heard or read that his Mother is there.

This small team of priests and sisters runs the normal life of the parish, as well as the abnormal life of this particular parish - thousands of pilgrims, requests for places to stay, information sessions in many languages, petitions, serving in the repository, confessions, cleaning the church every evening, cooking, cleaning, counselling, giving religious instruction to the primary school children, keeping up their hours of personal prayer, sleeping very little, available every moment to all comers, sharing all they have, even their little privacy. Recently they have extended their living quarters, taking over a few rooms in the church tower, so that the four sisters need no longer sleep in one room. This of course is unofficial, since the government refuses any kind of building permission. Houses are being built on all sides, and a communist party member has been allowed to build a restaurant near the church, but even though the parish has money set aside for toilets for the pilgrims, no permission can be had, and the three holes in the ground remain - for thousands. The pastor was fined for spreading gravel on the car park, and fined again for completing the air-conditioning of the church. Government pressure is one of their greatest trials.

But an even greater pressure comes from the local church authority, Bishop Pavao Zanic. When we remarked on the unusual absence of police, one of the parishioners commented, "The bishop is the policeman." Bishop Zanic has written that Medjugorje "must be extinguished." This conflict between loyalty to their bishop and belief in our Lady's urgent message is a cause of anguish to the parish, as no doubt the bishop's loyalty to the Church and his disbelief in the apparitions are a source of anguish for him.

Our days at Medjugorje were the last during which the five young people were allowed to appear publicly, before the bishop's ban. At Mass that Saturday evening I stayed at the back of the church, fortunate to be even inside as many were standing outside in the bitter wind. We began at six p.m. with the joyful and then the sorrowful mysteries of the rosary. Towards the end of this, the five young people - Vicka, Ivan, Marija, Ivanka, and Jakov - crossed the sanctuary from the sacristy to the small room opposite. No one is allowed to be there during the vision except one of the priests or sisters. Mass followed, and the door of the room remained closed. Then the five came out and led the congregation in saying the Creed, five "Our Father"s, "Hail Mary"s and "Glory Be"s. This was the last time. Then they left the sanctuary. Prayers followed, for healing of the sick, then the glorious mysteries of the rosary were said. It was by then nine p.m.

As we returned to the parish house we met Marija and Vicka. Both remembered us, and Vicka made a little rush of joy to greet Father Bob.She is obviously suffering and her face has changed; she is a little more withdrawn, though as animated as ever in conversation. Vicka has an inoperable cyst of the brain, between the cerebrum and the cerebellum; it debilitates her and gives her terrible headaches. She has seen doctors frequently and receives regular medical treatment. At present, Vicka remains at home for most of the evening apparitions; our Lady comes to her in her room at the same time that she comes to the others assembled in the parish rectory-convent. Although on her feet most of every day, seeing visiting pilgrims for long hours, Vicka finds herself often flat on her back with a fierce headache. Some in the parish have said that, at times when she is sick with a headache, she seems in some kind of trance or ecstasy, or "resting in the Spirit."

For over a year, until Easter week of 1985, the blessed Virgin spent time with Vicka, describing to her her whole life. Vicka has written down that story of Mary's life just as Mary told it to her. Our Lady has instructed her to give what she has written to a certain priest whom Vicka knows, but has not yet told her when to give it to him. At present, our Lady is daily giving Vicka information about future world events.

Palm Sunday was a cold, cloudy day. Father Bob spent part of the day talking with Fathers Tomislav Pervan and Slavko. I was able to spend the day praying and making the Stations of the Cross up the mountain. At eleven-thirty in the morning we had the parish Mass with a procession of palms - or, rather, of olive-branches. Behind the priests came the tiny equivalents of the Hebrew children, followed by the women, then the men. At this sort of parish Mass the people keep the old custom of women kneeling in the left-hand benches, men on the right. All had brought olive branches from their own trees. My neighbours quickly passed me small branches. We walked in procession around the outside of the church. Then came the singing of the Passion of our Lord.

Towards five I made my way to the parish house. There we were told that the children would be in the house that evening for their meeting with our Lady, instead of in the church, partly because a video film was to be made. Suddenly, Father Bob and I were bundled into Father Slavko's room, where the five young people and the four film crew were gathered. Two of the sisters joined us and Father Tomislav Pervan. It was about forty minutes before the usual time of our Lady's appearing. Father Bob was asked to introduce each mystery of the rosary, and Sister Janja would translate into Croatian. We sat as best we could fit, on the floor, on Father Slavko's couch-bed, on chairs. Vicka was next to Father Bob and myself. Introducing the fourth sorrowful mystery, Jesus carries his cross, Father Bob prayed that we would receive the grace to accept the cross and to carry it out of love. As Sister Janja translated this, Vicka bent forward, putting her head in her hands. Jakov jumped up and ran to comfort her, trying to make her raise her head.

We finished the rosary, then the five positioned themselves facing the wall, to wait for our Lady. They began to pray the "Our Father" - and suddenly, as one, dropped to their knees. Our Lady was there. After a pause they prayed aloud, then were silent, though Vicka's lips were moving as she spoke rapidly and nodded her head. But there was no sound. After some minutes they came to themselves as though returning from far away. They made the sign of the cross, and got up from their knees. We left them with Father Tomislav Pervan, and went over to the church for Mass. Seeing that I could not possibly get into the church I went to the sacristy by the outside door. The five arrived soon afterwards and stayed in the sacristy for Mass. It was quite a mêlée at first as the many concelebrants put on their albs and the small altar boys their cottas and wide crimson collars. The men who would take up the collection were there too, and I recognized among them Ivan Ivankovic who spent time in prison for expressing his belief in the apparitions.

Out of doors, confessions were still going on in the chill evening wind. When the Mass began the sacristy cleared except for the sisters, the visionaries and myself. Jakov was as active as ever; Marija was absorbed. Ivanka has grown tall and has the strong, noble stature typical of one type of Croatian woman. Ivan and Vicka were at the back of the small room; Vicka was quick to see that no one was kneeling on the stone floor without a little mat.

Back at the house after Mass we met Sister Josipa Kordic, an old friend of Father Bob's, who was to be our interpreter. On receiving a telephone call from Sister Janja to say that we had arrived, Sister Josipa had come from many miles away to help us, as she speaks not only Croatian but also Italian and English. Sister Josipa, born in the parish, is a favorite of everyone.

With her help, we talked and prayed briefly with Jelena Vasilj and Marijana Vasilj, the two thirteen-year-old girls who see our Lady and who receive messages from her. Although they have the same last name - Vasilj is a quite commonly found name in the region - they are not related. They are, however, close friends.

Our Lady has been speaking to Jelena, in her heart, since 15 December 1982. A week later, an angel appeared to her and urged her to do penance and to pray. After another week, our Lady appeared to her, and she continues to appear to her and to speak to her daily. Mary has said to Jelena, "I come to you in a different way than to the others, not to reveal things to the world through you, but rather to lead you along the path of consecration. Everything that the other six have said is true. I am sorry that I cannot give you the ten secrets. Those are God's gift for them."

Later, Marijana Vasilj began to receive the same spiritual gifts as Jelena - visions of our Lady and words from her. Both girls have a strong gift of prophecy. Our Lady uses them to guide the parish prayer groups through prophecy.

Jelena and Marijana are shy. Jelena in particular is quite shy and strong-willed; although she is only thirteen years old, one can see the reserve and the character in her face. She had earlier made it known to Sister Josipa that she hoped we would spare her any interviewing. So we did not interview her.

We had intended to interview Ivanka that evening, but she told us through Sister Josipa that Monday would be better. She also indicated that she hates tape-recorders!

The last member of our group, Father Helmut Leonard, arrived that evening. He was a great asset, not only in himself, but because he could speak German (he is Austrian) to our host Jozo. Father Helmut, and Rafael, a Californian, were to study the prayer groups which our Lady is forming among the younger parishioners, and which she guides by means of messages given through some of the visionaries and through Jelena.

Monday was a sunny day. Father Bob continued his sessions with Father Slavko and the others, heard confessions and ministered to pilgrims. There were Masses through the day and information sessions for the groups in their own langauges. They came from Italy, Germany, Spain, U.S.A., England, Ireland, Canada.

After the evening Mass the five young people did not lead the Creed and the other prayers but remained in the small room. We went in there to interview Ivanka with Sister Janja as interpreter. We did not use the tape-recorder, but I took notes. Ivanka is a pretty, tall young woman with long straight hair. She has a mature poise, much feminine warmth, and great life in her eyes and in her gestures. Ivanka explained that though usually she lives at Mostar, about an hour's drive away, just now her family were at their house in the village of Bijakovici (one of the five villages which make up the parish of Medjugorje), because they were working in their fields. Ivanka has finished school. Her mother died just before the apparitions of our Lady began. She lives with her father, who worked in Germany until recently but has now returned home after an accident, an older brother, Mario, a younger sister, Daria, and her grandmother. Her grandmother is seventy-eight years old, so Ivanka does much of the housework.

Ivanka described a typical day. When the family get up, they pray together before going off to work or to school. Ivanka makes breakfast and cleans the house. When we passed by one day she was outside the house doing the laundry. Sister Janja told us, "Ivanka is a great worker." Monday to Saturday there is field work. In the course of the day the family say the fifteen mysteries of the rosary and a long song/poem of reparation to Jesus.

Asked about her future, Ivanka says it will be whatever God gives her; just now, she does not know, but if God calls her to the religious life she is ready. Of prayer she said that she feels completely near to God, and talks to Jesus in her own words. We asked if she ever prays silently; she responded, "When I look at Jesus on the cross, I cry." Asked if she were ever distracted in prayer, she laughed and said that she was embarrassed to tell this to Father Vlasic, thinking she could not be normal to be distracted after having seen the blessed Virgin. We asked Ivanka what she would say to other young people about prayer. her answer was, "Pray with your heart. That's all."

Just as we finished talking, the prayers in the church finished, and the vision room was suddenly flooded with pilgrims. Seeing Ivanka, they all mobbed her. Father Bob and I were trying to get her out, but she was undismayed, passing through the crowd, friendly but purposeful.

As we reached the sacristy, Sister Janja told Father Rafael, Father Bob and me to go to the top of Mount Krizevac. For some time our Lady has been instructing several prayer groups in the parish. One is led by Ivan. Those of this group who live locally meet each Monday,

Wednesday and Friday night at whatever place and time our Lady indicates. At first it was always Mount Krizevac, but crowds began to follow them, using torches. The police sent over helicopters with searchlights, for religious gatherings are illegal outside churches. So the location is never known until the evening, and no one is permitted to go, except the group. Ivan, Marija and Vicka are part of this group.

It was 9.05 p.m., twenty minutes' walk to the foot of the mountain, then the steep climb over the rocks. Fathers Bob, Rafael and I set off along the road at a great rate, not daring to use a torch in the darkness, but helped by the light of the Easter moon. As we began to climb the winding path, Father Rafael, much younger than we are, raced ahead. After some minutes, though it was a chill night, Father Bob took off his hat, then his overcoat, then his jacket. Out of breath, I gasped, "We're almost there." We stopped briefly to see how far we still had to go, and realized we had come less than half way up the mountain. Groaning we pressed on. Breathless and with legs like jelly we reached the top, with five minutes to spare.

A small group of young men and women were sitting on rocks, looking out over the dark, light pricked plain below, as they prayed and sang. We were surprised to see that Vicka had managed the climb.

After a while all turned to kneel facing the cross, praying the "Our Father", "Hail Mary" and "Glory Be". Suddenly there was silence. Our Lady was there, seen only by Marija, Ivan and Vicka, through the other young people of the group apparently have different degrees of awareness of her presence. Some are aware of a diffuse light; some have a strong sense of her being there. There was complete silence for about ten minutes, the only sound, the night wind. As Marija afterwards remarked, our Lady stays much longer than she does in the apparitions at the church. At one moment during the vision, Marija, Ivan and Vicka prayed aloud, then were silent. As Mary left, they reached forward as though to detain her, and there was a murmured "Mother".

The group prayed in silence for a while, then took it in

turns to lead the "Our Father," etc. Then, singing, they walked up the steps to the cross, kissed it, genuflected, and then gathered at the lee side out of the wind. Ivan spoke into a tape-recorder held by one of the boys, while another took notes. He paused to check points with Vicka and Marija. Marija told us that our Lady had said she prayed for all who were there, and to go in peace. We sang "Alabare". "Andiamo," said Vicka in Italian, and we turned to go. Marija insisted on taking my arm for the descent. It made it much more difficult for me to pick my way over the rocks, but I appreciated her intention! Father Bob and I were thus able to talk with her as she speaks quite a little Italian.

Marija told us that she loves to go up Mount Krizevac to pray there at sunrise - then she said, "The sun rises in my heart." But recently she has been very ill, and now has a weak heart. But our Lady has told her, "If you wish to have a good heart, just want it and you will have it." Marija added, "I would rather have a new one."

The rest of the group waited for us at the foot of the hill. Someone passed round pieces of chocolate, then we went off singing quietly.

Tuesday. We waited for Sister Josipa to arrive by bus, then set off with her to walk through the fields to the village of Bijakovici to interview Vicka, Marija and Jakov. As we walked along the field path, through the spring blossom, always in sight of the five scattered villages, the hill of the apparitions called Podbrdo, and the hill of the cross, Sister Josipa pointed out her village and told us this story: When she returned from serving in the United States, Sister Josipa was allowed to visit her home and friends. She stayed overnight with Marija's family, and was walking through the fields in the morning on her way to church, with Marija, when she looked up at the cross on Krizevac. There, standing by the cross, embracing it, was a white figure. She called Marija's attention to it. Together they watched as the figure slowly sank to its knees at the foot of the cross. The whole episode lasted about ten minutes. Marija asked the blessed Mother at their next meeting if it were she whom they had seen. Our

Lady replied that it was. This is just one of many "signs" which our Lady has said are "to confirm your faith."

As we neared Bijakovici we met Marija sitting on the grass minding a flock of sheep. She was wearing a grey jumper and brown denim trousers as she sat reading François Mauriac's *Life of Jesus* in a Croatian translation. She had not told us the day before that it was her birthday - her twentieth. Sister Josipa had brought her a rosary, one of those made of pressed rose petals. Marija told us, "Our Lady said to me 'Happy birthday,' and she gave me a message for my life." "What was the message?" Sister Josipa asked. "I'm a little jealous of my message," Marija answered, laughing. We wanted to photograph her with the sheep, so she caught up a lamb to hold, then passed it to me while she took my photo. Marija said she would go to the house and ask her younger sister Milka to mind the sheep when we were ready to interview her.

So we went to Vicka's house and found it mobbed by Italian women, every one of whom wanted to kiss Vicka on both cheeks. "Don't you know she is ill?" we asked. They did. Vicka kept smiling, and later each of the girls in turn told us that greeting the pilgrims is part of their prayer.

We went inside. The family were at work in the fields, and just the very old, deaf grandmother was at home. A friend was helping to prepare dinner. They pressed us to take coffee, but we declined, and sat at the table with Vicka who answered our questions animatedly.

A few times she jumped up to answer the telephone. Marija came in and went to help at the sink. At one point, during the translation, they both took the bread out of the oven. Vicka's little sister arrived home from school and sat beside us at the table.

Afterwards Marija led us up the street to her house. Her father called a greeting; her mother was in the kitchen and insisted we have tea, and delicious chocolate doughnuts freshly baked by Milka. "She will have to make some more!" said Marija. She knelt on a cushion beside the coffee table while we sat around. People kept knocking on the door - pilgrims, asking her prayers. A friend arrived, a young man, and then a grandson, baby Filippo staggered in and grabbed my pencil and notes. So the tape-recording is full of noises-off.

The door burst open and Jakov put his head in to say that he was going to Citluk, and could we interview him on his return. We agreed and set a time for the afternoon, to meet at the parish house. But when the time arrived that afternoon, there was no sign of Jakov. Sister Josipa telephoned to him: "Why didn't you come?" "Come up to my house," he responded.

Jakov's mother died a year ago; he lives with his aunt and her two little girls. Their house is one of the more prosperous of the village, tastefully furnished. Jakov told us that he had just had his fourteenth birthday; he looks younger.

There was yet another interview to come. We were to meet Ivan after Mass. He came into the sacristy - unwilling, and declining to go to the vision room where crowds might follow. So with Sister Janja we went to the parish house, Ivan glowering at the people waiting to photograph him. We thought it better not to usethe tape-recorder. But as the interview began, Ivan found that we were asking about what he really cares about - his prayer. He relaxed, and when eventually he left, someone who saw him go said, "Why! Ivan had a big smile on his face; I've never seen him smile like that before."

This is what twenty-year-old Ivan told us: He gets up at five, and prays for one and a half hours. Then he eats and starts work. At noon he prays for an hour, works again, and then before Mass at six, he likes to prepare himself in church. On Monday, Wednesday and Friday he goes with the prayer group to pray after church, at nine p.m. The other days he has supper, and then goes to his room to relax in prayer.

The work, he said, is seasonal work in the fields: tobacco, potatoes, vines. He has two younger brothers, so, being the eldest, he likes to help his parents.

Sometimes when he prays he puts a candle or some other light to reflect on a crucifix. The biggest help in his prayer is the Bible. He usually reads a passage or a psalm and enjoys meditating on it for a long time. "Often," he said, "I stay on the work *Jesus* or *Abba*; but I also have some prayers that the blessed Virgin has taught me. I meditate on those." A lot of his prayer is silent: "I hear only the birds singing." He likes to love and to adore. We asked him about distractions. "No," he said, "unless someone knocks on the door." Asked if his prayer were ever dry or anguished, he replied, "When I pray, I don't pray; but someone else prays in me - Jesus."

He replied with feeling to a question about spiritual direction and confession. "They are the biggest help," he said. "If I had no spiritual leader or director in my life, I don't know what would have happened to me. It is the source of growth." For reading he uses books which his spiritual director gives to him. He mentioned some titles: *Jesus Christ a Real Man* and *Introduction to the Prayer of the Heart*. We asked him if he had anything to say to young men of his own age who wanted to pray. Sister Janja who was translating changed the question to "anything to say to the world." Ivan's answer was a crisp "Nothing." Sister reformulated the question as we had asked it, and he replied, "Who *want* to pray? If they are looking for a way to pray, I would say that for me the Bible is the biggest help in my prayer. Praying with the Scriptures I experience the Lord - an experience which I wish all who pray would have. By meditating on the Bible, and with the tools of fasting and penance, everyone can grow in mature Christian living. What is most important," he added, "is that before beginning to pray, you do all you can to get peace; peace in which you can concentrate and have inner unity."

On Wednesday, Father Bob and I went to the neighbouring town of Vitina to see Father Tomislav Vlasic. Father Tomislav Vlasic, O.F.M., first went to Medjugorje on June 29, 1981, the sixth day of the apparitions. Soon afterwards he was transferred there to act as spiritual director to the "visionaries". On August 17, 1981, the local secret police and the military surrounded the rectory and arrested the pastor Father Jozo Zovko. Father Vlasic replaced him until Father Tomislav

Pervan was appointed. Pressure from the Bishop of Mostar recently forced the Franciscan superiors to move Father Vlasic to a neighbouring parish. Father Slavko Barbaric replaced him as spiritual director, but he continues to act as prayer group chaplain, driving in from Vitina.

An Irish gentleman and his invalid wife kindly took us to Vitina in their car. Mrs McMahon was one of many people, including Croatians, who reported seeing our Lady the previous evening at Mass, as the tabernacle was opened before Holy Communion.

The sun continues to spin at various times: we both saw it more than once. Marija told us that once when someone called to her to come because the sun was spinning, she went on her way saying, "Why should I bother to see the sun when I can see the blessed Virgin Mary?" The greatest signs, all are agreed, are the graces of prayer, of conversion and of neighborly love which so many receive and which are so evident in the people of Medjugorje. In 1931 there was such a feud among the villages of the parish, that five villagers were killed in the fighting, and it took five years to settle the quarrel. But these volatile people are now almost all converted. They live together in peace and co-operation.

3. Interviews

Most things in Medjugorje are dated as "since the *Gospa* came." Life changed for the five village communities, especially Medjugorje and Bijakovici which are on the "pilgrim road" - to the cross on Mount Krizevac and to the site of the apparitions, respectively. The families of the visionaries live in Bijakovici. It is their lives which have changed most dramatically. Their serenity is amazing. Vicka's mother says she has given Vicka to God. That is no euphemism, for Vicka, like Marija, is lost to the family as far as field-work and earning a living are concerned. And their house is continually mobbed. But more profoundly, giving Vicka to God entails watching her suffer. She has a benign cyst on the brain which is inoperable because it presses on a blood vessel. Vicka says she will never ask our Lady to cure her. Her pain is often intense. We asked Vicka about her day, and in particular about her prayer.

Vicka

She told us: "I pray the rosary more than any other prayer, though it pleases me very much to talk spontaneously to the Lord. But mostly, I pray the rosary. Some days I pray more, other days less. As a matter of fact, I can never spend a whole day in prayer. Really I cannot! Every day from the time I get up, I have to greet the pilgrims who come to see me. Sometimes they are here at six or seven o'clock. They want me to talk with them, and they recount their needs. Nobody wants to go away until they have seen me, because every one has needs. Practically, we cannot do any work, because we are always wanted. In fact, we could spend the whole day at the door receiving pilgrims. Very often the whole day passes in that way. My mother leaves me at home now. If I can manage some work and it isn't too difficult, I do it.

"Compared with what I was before, I like to pray - and I see that I am praying properly - from the heart. But I can't leave the people aside. One has to be involved. I do relate to God as my Father, but I must say I prefer to talk to Jesus. I am more open to him, and can say everything to him, though I don't see him. I take refuge in him; I feel him close; I trust him and he helps. I have many petitions - many people asking me to pray for them. Often I read the Psalms, and I always say the Magnificat after all other prayers."

Asked if our Lady helped her to learn to pray, Vicka replied robustly, "Of course she did! But I had to put some effort into learning. Our Lady often repeats that there is no need to wait for her to say everything, but that we should begin doing something. She wants to see that you are making some effort and that you are willing to pray. You don't have to wait for a message from our Lady, or stop there and say 'Our Lady has given me a message - finish!' I, and all of us, must practise the message. How can I hand it on to you if it remains only words?"

Vicka used to pray with the large prayer group. "I stopped going to the big group. Somehow there was a lot of meditation, and I'm not for big meditation. I can say even ten Rosaries, but I can't meditate much. It isn't that I'm distracted, but it seems to me, I'm not made for meditation. The Lord did not give me that gift. I must sincerely admit it!" But she continues to pray with Ivan's group, of which she said: "In a particular way our Lady encourages us this Lent to experience deeply the Way of the Cross. If we don't do it well she tells us immediately: 'Today I am not pleased with you. Improve, because you can do it much better.' Mainly, our Lady encourages us to continue in the way we have begun, and that we don't wait for her admonitions. Our Lady wants our group to really go ahead - to grow."

Spontaneously she spoke of our Lady: "Our Lady is a Mother; she loves us all. She will never reprimand anyone or shout at them. She is not at all strict. Her voice, her tender motherly manner incite one to pray. It is impossible to describe. You could understand only by taking my place and meeting our Lady."

Of suffering, Vicka said - and it is not pious words, but

painful experience: "Everything that God gives,, every cross, every suffering, should be accepted with wide open hands. And there must be patience, because only then can one see how joyful one is in experiencing all the crosses that God sends. Then one becomes even more joyful, and can even look for more suffering from God. God then gives more strength to endure. There is only one thing I could say to people who suffer: Be persevering, because God gives you suffering in order that you may know him better, the true God, and because he wants to show you that he is the only one true God and only one true Love who loves us all. Persevere - and know and love him better.

"This illness that God gives me, I offer as a particular way of prayer, because God does not want only prayers like the 'Our Father', 'Hail Mary', 'Glory be'. I give him everything that is in my heart, and also my suffering. I am glad that I can endure everything that God sends me, with love, that love which he gives me. And I can only be grateful to him."

Jakov.

Sister Josipa came as interpreter for the interview with Jakov. She and he carried on an animated conversation, so that we needed to ask little. Here is their exchange:

Sister Josipa: Jakov, tell us something about your day and what you do.

Jakov: It's like this: When I wake up in the morning I pray a bit, then, when it is time, I go to school. In school I do everything on the program. When classes finish I pop into church, at least sometimes. When I come home, and also during the day, I pray. If my aunt needs help, I help her, but if there is nothing, I go out to play. When the time comes to go to church, I prepare myself.

S.J. Do you pray together at home in the evenings?

J. We say the rosary, the seven "Our Fathers," Hail Mary"s and "Glory be"s, and then also five "Our Father"s. Then we pray for the Bishop and for the Holy Father.

S.J. Do you finish elementary school this year?

J. Yes

S.J. Where do you intend to go afterwards?

J. To one of the Citluk schools. I don't know exactly. I can choose. There are different trades and so on - many possibilities.

S.J. Do you like anything particular at school?

J. Yes, my companions, because we all pray together. On Friday to be exact, our class says the rosary.

S.J. The whole class?

J. Yes, all of them. But not only our class. Now the other classes also - on Monday the first grade and the fifth grade. One Friday we pray, and the fourth grade.

S.J. Is it ever difficult for you to pray?

J. Prayer is never difficult for me. Sometimes, particularly when there are many people coming here, I get distracted. But I try to be patient. Prayer is the most precious thing to me in my whole life.

S.J. Do you include the people who come to you and recommend themselves to you?

J. I do that at church. I recommend them to our Lady. We always pray with our Lady. We say the "Our Father" and the "Glory be" with her. She tells us to pray.

S.J. What about reading?

J. Yes, I do read. I get different books at school, so-called required readings. Whether you want to or not, you have to!

S.J. Do you read the Bible?

J. First I read something, then I reflect on it. God gives us his message and I must think about it. After that I thank God for everything he has done. I think that every prayer is a conversation with God - from heart to heart.

S.J. What do you think prayer means to those your age - ones as young as you?

J. I haven't spoken about it with them.

S.J. Look, now you have an opportunity! You won't see those who will read the book that Father Bob and Sister Lucy will write. What would you like to say to them? Any message?

J. To the young ones?

S.J. Yes.

J. I'd like them really to pray. That is the most necessary thing. Then they should go for religious instruction, and they should obey.

S.J. When you say "obey" whom do you mean?

J. Parents and religious teachers. And they should go to Mass.

S.J. Do you find the religious instructions interesting?

J. Just now it is most interesting. The priests are explaining the history of the Church in Croatia.

Marija

Our Lady has called Marija to "much, much prayer." She participates in two prayer groups as well as receiving messages for the parish group. She spoke to us about some of the activities coming from the prayer groups:

"Recently, before Christmas, our Lady told us to go to those who are abandoned, who are lonely; to visit them. We, the majority of the group, should help them as we can. We went to some of these people, thinking 'They will never accept us, because they might think that Our Lady has sent us!' When we came to a certain woman, she exclaimed, 'You are sent by our Lady!' She welcomed us with joy, though we had thought that she would say, 'I can still help myself. I don't need your help.' We took a guitar and sang a bit to her, and she joined in. Then we prayed with her. The next day we came again. We girls cleaned her room, and the boys chopped firewood for her. She now looks forward to when we will come again. In fact, she doesn't have anyone, of her family. When we go there she tells us her problems. She talks about her sheep, and so on. Sometimes I think to myself, 'Poor sheep: when she dies, the sheep will be left alone.'

"Similarly we collect clothes and send them down to Kosovo where there are many poor people. We are doing all this on the initiative of our Lady. Of ourselves, certainly we wouldn't do it.

"Last night we had a meeting for half an hour. We were reflecting about the coming work in the fields - that during that time people won't have time for prayer. And we thought that it would be a good idea if we as a prayer group met for adoration from nine o'clock to midnight before the Blessed Sacrament exposed, for those who cannot pray because of work.

"We get together three times a week. It used to be twice a week, but our Lady told us twice was not enough, because she wishes to form us."

Asked about her day, Marija said: "Besides housework, I pasture the sheep. And when work comes in the vineyards and tobacco-fields, I will do that. But just now there isn't that kind of work. And I do try to find some time for my personal prayer, when I pray alone. Besides, I participate in two prayer groups. For instance, at this time, our Lady wishes us to meditate on the five wounds of Jesus. I do it very eagerly. Otherwise too, I pray before the cross, and whenever I pray, I try to have a cross at hand. No matter how I contrive my plans, and I do make some plans, as I was advised by some friends, there has to be room in them for the people who will come to visit me, and for prayer with them. More and more people are coming during the day, and I have to leave many things to be done over-night. Talking with the people can be a prayer, but sometimes I feel I simply must disappear and retire into solitude, and pray.

"Vicka said that she likes best to say the rosary. I don't think I could say the same thing for myself. I gladly say a rosary, but I think, nevertheless, that I prefer to meditate. I like every sort of prayer, but preferably I read some verses from the Bible, and then I meditate. I feel I need exactly that, because from one day to the next, one talks and talks; the people ask and ask! After that I feel that I simply need that kind of prayer, and it suits me.

"In the same way I eagerly read the psalms, and I offer all this in spirit to the Lord, and also all those intentions people have given me. Many people come with big problems, and after they have told me those problems, I feel uneasy, but they have relaxed. Somehow it all remains in me. Afterwards I try to offer it to God - all the problems of those people - because I know that once I offer it to God, it will not remain in me. But sometimes I still think about those things - it is like a film passing before my eyes. But when I really offer God everything without reserve, then I feel silence in the depth of my heart.

"Each time it's difficult to pray, I remember our Lady, then it isn't difficult any more. Our Lady says 'PRAY' - if only you could hear how she says it - then you would be able to understand me completely!"

About reading, Marija told us: "I like to read about the experiences of the saints - biographies. Recently I haven't read anything except Holy Scripture, because I don't have time, and besides, other reading somehow does not agree with me. Before, I used to read a lot - even magazines, anything available. Then later, when I read a little of that sort of thing, I felt a kind of fear. When our Lady told us to accept everyone as a brother and as a sister, I again started opening myself. Often when the bishop and different newspapers wrote against Medjugorje, I simply rejected it all, and I didn't want to read it any more. I talked about it with Archbishop Franic when he visited us here, and I told him that I don't want to read things written against Medjugorje. But he told me that I must read those writings. 'You will build yourself up through it,' he said. 'You will understand that someone whom you would like to reject, you must accept and pray for.' Since then, I have begun reading those reports again."

All the young people are very involved in their village communities. Vicka had said, and all the others confirmed it, that the other visionaries are not their only friends, "though they are something special to me." Both Marija and Vicka singled out their prayer groups in particular. Vicka added: "Regarding other people who go to church, and who pray, I feel them very close to me. They are all from our village. Nobody looks at me strangely, because they all pray, so I'm not something special. They accept and obey the messages, and do what our Lady asks. If they didn't, all this would not go smoothly. It would be different."

It used to be different according to Marija: "Since the apparitions we are all united. It is true that it applies especially to us in the prayer group - in which we are sixty three. But I am on good terms with everybody. There are some people who are less active - they have some obstacles - they are studying in Mostar or in Sarajevo. The rest of us here are really united. Our Lady has united us very much, and has insisted that we keep together, and work together. Formerly there was disunity."

Marija makes no secret of her call to the religious life. "From the very beginning of the apparitions something was growing in me, and what I am thinking now, formerly I couldn't even dream of! I had actually determined on a direction completely the opposite. But now, from day to day I feel a certain vocation which is being consolidated more and more. This vocation is leading me to a convent. I really do feel that God wants me there but how, and in what way, I don't yet know. The way I regarded the sisters before - I couldn't even have dreamed of going that way!"

4. The Communities

In April 1985 Sister Lucy and Father Bob Faricy together with Fathers Helmut Leonard and Rafael Luevano, went to Medjugorje as a team to study what kind of communities our Lady was forming in the parish. This chapter states briefly and schematically what we found.

We had some difficulty in acquiring information on the various groups. To begin with, Medjugorje is a domestic farming community, a relatively unstructured society. Any grouping in Medjugorje has, by the nature of the overall society and tradition there, a fairly nebulous structure. For example, when some of us tried to fix times for appointments, Sister Janja Boras pointed out to us, smiling, that "this is not the United States where you do that kind of thing." Father Slavko Barbaric, one of the principal agents of community-building in the parish, a priest with wide experience in different cultures, in our conversations with him strongly played down the statistics and the structures of the groups, and stressed the importance of the motivation and of the spirit of the participants.

As Father Rafael put it, the members of any of the communities "are wonderfully caught up in the spirit of their community experience, not in its structure." The different communities, of course, have norms; but these norms do not govern the groups - they serve them.

Furthermore, the long history of Turkish occupation and persecution of Catholics in Bosnia-Herzegovina has left a tradition of suspicion of those who inquire and of resistance to any interference. In the present situation, this attitude appears quite realistic. The Yugoslavian government, and in particular the local government, is strongly opposed to everything religious that goes on in the parish. The local communist government and police force understand the apparitions of Our Lady as a serious threat to all that communist ideology stands for. The church in Medjugorje is, therefore, a persecuted church. And only with great reticence do Catholics give out to anyone information that those who persecute the church might find useful.

Father Slavko and the communities

Father Slavko Barbaric, the spiritual director of the young people who see Our Lady, and the chief spiritual animator of the parish, has a doctorate in adult religious education from the University of Freiburg in Switzerland. He wrote his doctoral dissertation only a few years ago, on conversion. He says that the important thing about conversion is to sustain it, to keep it alive. The various prayer communities in the parish helps to do that.

In Saint James' parish, Father Slavko says, "We have an ideal situation; everyone has experienced conversion." He and the other priests have to take care of the continuing forward movement of conversion in the people of the parish. "It is like a great flowing river; every one here moves in this river." The priests try to create a spiritual environment that will sustain the movement of ongoing conversion in the parishioners. The various prayer groups and communities and the different seminars contribute to the existence of that environment, to the movement of the great river of continuing conversion.

As the spiritual director of the young people who see and speak with the Blessed Virgin every day, Father Slavko is in many ways the key man in the parish. Further since he speaks several languages fluently, he has much contact with the pilgrims, who come in always increasing numbers. An intense and efficient worker, Father Slavko spends long hours daily in parish work, guiding the five young people, working with groups, speaking to pilgrims, helping visiting priests. We saw him frequently between the rectory and the church, walking quickly, or stopping to speak to visitors.

"The groups," he says, "are like posts in a fence; without the posts, the fence collapses." Those in the various groups go more deeply into the movement of conversion, into the flow of the great river, and "they sustain the parish community."

The seminars

Father Slavko, during our stay in Medjugorje, is giving a six-week seminar on the spiritual life. During the six weeks of the seminar, a temporary community is formed in which the participants learn to pray together better and to share their lives at a spiritual level.

A theology professor from Zagreb gave the first seminar a few years ago, from after Christmas until January second, every day from morning to evening. Father Slavko has given several seminary, of varying contents and to different groups of people in the parish. For the present seminar he uses a book written by the same theology professor, a manual for use precisley in giving a seminar on the spiritual life.

Father Helmut took part in a seminar meeting. This seminar meets every Sunday and Wednesday evening, after the Mass and the rosary, in the rectory basement. Here is an excerpt from Father Helmut's notes from the meeting:

> In this seminar the participants learn to meet God in their everyday life and to share their spiritual lives with one another. Husbands and wives learn to share spiritually at a deeper level. Neighbors learn to share their spiritual lives.
>
> This evening there are twenty people sitting in a circle. Five couples take part in the seminar, but two of the husbands have to work tonight in the factory in Citluk, a town a few miles away. They will learn tomorrow from the men here tonight.

The prayer group

About sixty young people, along with four older women, make up what is called simply "the prayer group." The average age is about twenty. Some of the young people have not yet finished secondary school; others have, and most of these work in the grape and the tobacco fields. The group meets on Tuesday, Thursday and Saturday evenings at nine, after Mass and the rosaries. The meetings have no fixed format; they usually last about two hours. There are no elected leaders or committees.

Marija is the only one of the young people to whom Our Lady has appeared daily since 1981 who belongs to the prayer group. Sister Janja says that since the group began the change in the lives of those in it has been remarkable. "They were good before, but now they are growing in faith and in life," she says. "Sometimes I participate in the prayer group; we speak quite openly about our misunderstandings and our faults and even our sins. They feel that God knows them perfectly and that Our Blessed Mother is very near to them, so that it seems natural to be open with one another. I think that Our Blessed Mother is very pleased because they do pray, they do fast, they do work in the parish and to help the needy. It is incredible."

The group began in this way: Near the end of May 1983, Our Lady asked Jelena Vasilj, then eleven years old, to begin a prayer group which Our Lady herself would guide. She said:

> I want a prayer group here. I will lead the group and give it instruction for holiness of life. Through this in struction others in the world will learn to consecrate themselves. I allow one month for this group to form. But tell them the conditions of belonging to it. To begin with, they have to renounce everything and put themselves entirely in God's hands. They must renounce all fear; abandonment to God has no place for fear. All the difficulties that they meet will work for their spiritual growth and for the glory of God... I prefer young people because married people have family and work obligations. But everyone who wants to take part in this program can do so, at least partially. I will lead this group.

The blessed Virgin said that she would guide the group through Jelena, and that the group should have a priest. Father Tomislav Vlasic has acted as chaplain for the group from the beginning.

Father Rafael asked Sister Janja if the group were "charismatic" or not. She answered, "I would say they are charismatic because 'charisma' means 'grace'. They are open. Here, you can call everyone 'charismatic'. It is different than in the United States." Father Rafael asked, "How do they pray when they are together!" Sister Janja responded, "They meditate in silence; they pray aloud spontaneously; sometimes they pray the rosary."

The blessed Virgin has taught them how to pray together, and how to share together spiritually. In September 1984 our Lady told the group to meet together in twos, outside the time of the prayer meeting. After some minutes of prayer, they should share together what is in their hearts about God, faith, difficulties or problems. During Lent she asked them to meet every two or three days. After a while she instructed them not to talk together about anything and everything, but of things concerning faith, prayer, peace. That kind of sharing, she said, is also prayer. Father Helmut reported: "Every day I saw young people of the village on Mount Krizevac, especially in the early morning. Usually they were in pairs, praying the rosary aloud, or talking with each other, or in silence."

Our Lady gave Jelena the conditions for membership in the prayer group. Each person should give himself or herself completely to God. Each should remain in the group for at least four years and be obedient to the guidance of Mary who speaks through messages which she gives to Jelena. No group member can make any lifetime commitment, such as marriage or religious life or a profession, until after the four years, and they are to avoid any romantic attachments.

Each prayer group member has the obligation to pray at least three hours daily; those who work or who go to school should pray at least half an hour in the morning and half an hour in the evening. They are also committed to daily Mass. Our Lady told the group at the beginning, "Do not be surprised that I ask this. You are not able to fulfill your duties because you pray too little." And she added, "When there are difficulties, I will ask you to fast and pray more." One day, during a prayer meeting, she told the group:

> You have begun to pray for three hours. But why do you keep looking at your watches? You are too taken up

with how you should do your work and get it finished. I want to tell you that you will never finish it that way. You must let the Spirit lead you in a deep way. Leave your worries aside. Offer your time to God. You will be able to get everything done, and you will even have time to spare.

Furthermore, they fast on bread and water on Wednes days and Fridays, go to Mass and Communion daily, and consecrate themselves every day to the hearts of Jesus and Mary.

They do their best to love everyone that they have any contact with, including any who oppose them in any way. They try to be helpful to all around them. They give no place to anger or resentment in their lives. And they ask God every day to pour out his Holy Spirit on the whole world.

The group began with a one-month period of prayer and fasting during which each person made a decision whether or not to respond personally to this call from Mary, whether or not to make the four-year commitment. Then the group started under the guidance of our Lady. Six weeks later, our Lady told the group through Jelena:

Now listen carefully. You have decided to follow Jesus' way, to consecrate yourselves totally to him. When someone tries to follow God unreservedly, Satan comes and attempts to steer him away from what he has begun. This is a time of testing. Satan will tell you, "You are doing too much. Why not just be like other Christians? There is no need to pray and to fast." I tell you that you must persevere in your prayer and in your fasting. Satan can do nothing to those who abandon themselves entirely to God.

There are sixty-three persons in the group. The group does not make plans for its future, since it depends completely on the guidance of the blessed Virgin Mary who directs through Jelena.

It seems clear that the prayer group is a kind of four-year formation program. Above all, it is a school of prayer. Mary has guided and taught the group through Jelena from the beginning, and more recently also through Marijana. The prophecies that come to them through Mary frequently stress the imprortance of prayer and teach how to pray. What matters is not so much the time spent or the number of prayers said, but to pray with love, from the heart. Mary has taught the group how to pray the "Our Father" slowly. She has taught them a special way to say the "Jesus rosary", traditional in Croatia. We have added it, the way Mary taught it, in the final chapter of this book.

Our Lady's Group

Three of those who have met with the blessed Virgin Mary daily since 1981, Ivan, Vicka and Marija, belong to "Our Lady's Group," along with twelve other young people. They range in age from sixteen to twenty-four; most of them are single, but there are a few married couples. This group meets three times a week; during the meeting, Our Lady appears to Ivan, Vicka and Marija, and gives the group instructions and guidance through them.

The group meets to pray together. It is a prayer group, and also clearly a formation group. Mary is forming these young people in prayer, in community, and in the whole Christian life.

During the regular evening apparitions, three times a week, our Lady tells the young people where she will meet the group and at what time. The times vary, and so do the places. Usually the appointment is for quite late at night in some remote place. The meeting is only for the group, not generally open to visitors.

The real leader of this group is the blessed Virgin Mary. But, after her, Ivan seems to be the natural leader. A little below average height, slender and nice-looking, he usually says very little. His face rarely shows much expression. He has an unusual dignity.

Ivan still hopes to be a priest and has all the signs of a genuine priestly vocation. He entered a junior seminary but could not keep up with the academic work, not, it seems, was he understood by the superiors.

Other groups
There are many other groups in Saint James' parish; no one seems to know how many. Most of them are small, informal groups that meet daily, or two or three times a week, to pray together and to share spiritually. Some of these groups stem from the "prayer group".

From time to time, temporary groups form under the leadership of one of the parish priests. Besides the seminars under the direction of Father Slavko, there currently exists, for example, a group that studies Franciscan spirituality under Father Pero. Father Slavko told us that, if there were more priests in the parish, they could do more.

The family as community: staying at Jozo's
The coming of the blessed Virgin Mary to Medjugorje has revolutionized the life of most of the families of the parish. One such family is that of Jozo Vasilj. Jozo's house is small and simply furnished in the local style. It lies at the foot of Mount Krizevac, about a twenty-minute walk from Saint James's church and the rectory.

Many of the men in Medjugorje have worked for several years in Germany. Jozo worked there for six years before the birth of his first child.

Here are some of our impressions of Jozo and his family, and of how our Lady has influenced the life of a typical young family in the parish. Jozo and his wife Marica have four children: Ivana is ten years old; their son Mate is seven; Angelina is five; and Marija is two. Jozo's mother, Anda, lives with them - a strong, quiet woman, she smiles often. Anda often takes care of the children; she helps with the work in the fields; she takes care of the family's two cows.

Jozo is outgoing and, like his mother, almost always smiling. He seems stong, independent, and happy. His wife Marica is quiet, slim, hard-working and loving. Marica keeps house and does the cooking; like the other housewives of the region, she bakes her own bread and makes her own cheese, a mild white cheese with a distinctive flavour.

The oldest and youngest girls are, like Jozo, strong, smiling, outgoing. Mate and his sister Angelina are like their mother, not shy but somewhat retiring, quiet, loving.

Jozo has grape and tobacco fields. He and Marica work in the fields according to the seasons. Sometimes Jozo uses his car as a taxi to drive pilgrims to Split or to Dubrovnik to catch an airplane.

Like the other Catholics in Bosnia-Herzegovina, the people of Saint James' parish have not forgotten the four centuries of religious persecution under Turkish rule. Although the Turks left one hundred years ago, the bonds forged under them among Catholics and with the Franciscan priests remain. During the persecutions, when other priests fled, the Franciscans went underground, into lay clothes, and stayed with the people. Many Franciscans were martyred by the Turks. "The priest was our brother," Jozo says; "he laughed with us and he wept with us; he was one of us." Jozo explains the love that the people here have for their priests. "What the priest says is, for us, the truth; and what he says, we do."

Medjugorje lies, along with Citluk and other villages, in a broad highland valley surrounded by mountains. The clouds frequently break over the mountains and pour down thunder-storms and hail on the valley. Up until 1933, hailstorms did much damage to the grape and tobacco crops, and lightning occasionally killed someone. In 1933, the parish celebrated the anniversary of Jesus' death and resurrection by building a cross on the highest mountain nearby, Mount Krizevac. They built the cross not only in celebration and thanksgiving, but also as a prayer that God protect them from damage from storms. The whole village participated in the building of the large concrete cross. They carried it, piece by piece, up the mountain. It is their cross.

Since 1933, there has been no more crop damage from hail or other storms, and no one has been hit by lightning. "When a storm starts to gather," Jozo says, "and there is danger of hail, we ring the church bells; when the bells begin to ring, you can see the clouds change direction and unload on the hills around us, sparing the village." Jozo says this in a matter-of-fact way, like the sound and down-to-earth farmer that he is.

Since our Lady has come to the village, Jozo tells us, he has understood from her messages that every husband and father is a priest for his family. Now he reads the Bible every evening with his two older children. Everyone listens. In the small house, kitchen and dining room and living room are all one room. While Marica feeds the two smaller children on one side of the room, Jozo sits on the other side with Ivana and Mate, reading to them. "They also hear the Bible read in church," he says, "but at home, from their father, it sounds different - closer to them, more direct; and they can ask questions - I answer as well as I can." Recently, Jozo has begun to buy illustrated bible-story books; the children love them.

Since the *Gospa* (Croatian for "Lady") has come ...." Jozo speaks of the *Gospa*, of our Lady, as one might speak of a person who has come to live in the village and whose presence has transformed everything. For Jozo, our Lady has specially chosen his village according to the same special providence of God that protects the village from lightning and from hail. She lives there among them. She guides the village. She knows them and helps them.

Even before the *Gospa* came, Jozo's family prayed together every morning and every evening. But now they pray more, and more from the heart. After the three older children have gone to school in the morning, while the youngest is still asleep, Jozo and Marica and Anda say their traditional morning prayers together. They add, as our Lady has instructed all in the parish to do, seven "Our Father"s, seven "Hail Mary"s, and seven "Glory be"s. They say their evening prayers after the children have gone to bed, adding the rosary, and also prayers in honor of Jesus' five wounds. They also pray before and after meals, and daily with the whole family together they say the rosary.

The three adults in the family fast twice a week on bread and water, as do almost all the Catholic families in Medjugorje. The intensity of spiritual life in Jozo's house could seem unusual. In fact, it is typical of the Catholic families of the village. In prayer and fasting, Jozo's family seem about average for Medjugorge.

Every day, at least one member of Jozo's family goes to the evening Mass, taking part too in the prayers before and after Mass. Jozo himself goes at least three times during the week, and also of course on Sunday. "Now is a bad time,"Jozo says, explaining why he cannot go to Mass every day in this season. Most of the villagers have to work especially long hours in the fields while the soil is humid and soft, before it goes dry and hard. It is the time for plowing and planting.

Jozo finds that he spends perhaps less time now with his friends. Before the *Gospa* came, often on Sundays Jozo organised a feast with his friends. Some families roasted a pig in the open air while the others went to the first Mass. Then they alternated for the second Mass. It was a joyful time, says Jozo, and friends really stuck together. "Sometimes I'm afraid that this new thing that began with the apparitions separates us; we don't get together as much as we used to." And then he adds, "But, after all, now we have the *Gospa* with us."

Medjugorje is a village of prayer. Father Ivan Dugancic, the novice master at the Franciscan monastery a few miles from Medjugorje, is a member of the commission appointed by the local bishop to investigate the apparitions. He tells us about a skeptical priest who wanted the young people who see our Lady to ask her, "Why should it be better to pray here rather than somewhere else?" The answer that the young people gave him from our Lady was, "It is better to pray here, because here people pray better." The spirit of prayer permeates the atmosphere in the village. Families like Jozo's, hundreds of them, create a stong matrix of prayer. You can almost feel it in the air.

"Prayer," Jozo says to us, expressing the conviction of the whole village, "is the most powerful force in the world for overcoming difficulties and bringing peace."

5. The Cross at Medjugorje

The cross at the top of Mount Krizevac stands over Medjugorje. And it stands symbolically for the suffering there now.

The church in Saint James' parish, Medjugorje, is a suffering church. Medjugorje suffers in the structure of the cross. The people of the parish suffer not only from persecution by a communist government that strongly opposes the presence of our Lady and the devotion shown her. They suffer also because of the opposition of the local bishop.

Officially, in his capacity as bishop, Bishop Pavao Zanic, residing at Mostar, the nearest large town, has made no statement, issued no condemnation. But unofficially he has heatedly made his views widely known: the apparitions are a hoax, the priests of the parish are charlatans, the young people who claim to see Mary are robots manipulated by the wily Franciscans. (*The Present Position, Not Official, of the Episcopal Curia of Mostar, Regarding the Events at Medjugorje.* By Bishop Pavao Zanic. October 30, 1984).

Recently, in fact, police persecution has eased considerably. At present, the police neither harass, insult, nor search pilgrims. On recent visits, we found no police, at least none in uniform, on the parish grounds. The usual police spies, of course, come regularly to the evening services, but they cause no trouble. The communists seem to have confidence that Bishop Zanic will close down the whole affair of the apparitions and the pilgrimages. One local police chief shook his finger at two priests recently, on two separate occasions, saying, "Why do you not obey your bishop? *He* does not believe in the apparitions."

This chapter takes up how Church officials besides the pastor and the other parish priests view Medjugorje. How does the Holy See look at Medjugorje? The other bishops of Yugoslavia? What has the Bishop of Mostar said and written, albeit completely unofficially, about Medjugorje?

And what lies behind and below the conflict between the bishop and the Franciscans?

The background: Turks, Franciscans, bishop.

In 1463 the Turks under Sultan Mohammed II occupied Bosnia and Herzegovina, forcibly converting many Catholics to Islam. Those who clung to the Catholic faith underwent severe persecution and, sometimes, martyrdom. Most of the diocesan clergy, including the bishops, fled from Bosnia-Herzegovina. The Franciscan Order remained. Wearing secular dress and keeping secret their priestly identity, the Franciscans said Mass and ministered clandestinely.

Before long, the Franciscans obtained from Sultan Mohammed II a charter allowing them to minister. And they obtained from the Holy See permission to act as parish priests - a privilege they retain today, and part of the cause of the problems with the diocesan clergy and the bishop. By the time the Turks left, many families who had been converted to Islam had returned to Roman Catholicism.

Bosnia, helped by Serbia and Montenegro, revolted against the Turks in 1875; Turkish rule ended in 1878. The prinicipal European powers showed great interest, and finally in 1908 Emperor Franz Josef annexed both Bosnia and Herzegovina to the Hapsburg empire. The Turks had gone home, but Bosnia-Herzegovina had passed from one master to another.

At the end of the First World War, with the breakup of the Hapsburg empire, the nation of Yugoslavia took shape under a Serbian dynasty. The Croatian-speaking Catholic population of Croatia and of Bosnia-Herzegovina looked on this new unity as one of equal partners. But the Orthodox Serbs saw it as a further extension of the kingdom of Serbia. Even today, Croatian-speaking Catholics harbour some resentment against Serbian domination. Yugoslavia's capital, Belgrade, is Serbian. The Serbs speak a language they call "Serbo-Croatian." One learns in Herzegovina not to say "Serbo-Croatian." "They are two different different languages," we were informed, "Serbian and Croatian; the cultures and the languages are similar, but not the same."

During World War II, savage conflict broke out, especially in Herzegovina, between the Catholic Croats and the Orthodox Serbs, in the Croatian state, including Bosnia-Herzegovina, set up by the Hitler and Mussolini dictatorships and welcomed enthusiastically by the Croatian clergy. The Croatian government of this new state asserted its allegiance to the Roman Catholic Church and set about eliminating all the Orthodox Serbs. The Catholic Church saw an opportuninty for converts; the rule from Belgrade had ceased, the Serbian hegemony was over, and Catholicism could flourish. The worst atrocities took place in Herzegovina, in the Mostar diocese. Thousands of Serbs fled, and thousands were brutally murdered.

Even today, since the possibility arose of Pope John Paul II visiting Yugoslavia, the Serbian Orthodox bishops have been insisting that the Pope should make the Croatian Catholic bishops apologize for the atrocities committed against the Serbs under the wartime Pavelic regime. Croat bishops are eager for reconciliation between Serbs and Croats, but feel that such an act of contrition would imply that the Catholic Church rather than the Pavelic regime had been persecuting the Serbs. (Besides, nothing has been said on the Serbian side about any apology for the killing of Croats during and after the war). (see *The Tablet,* London, "Politics of a Visit", 3 March, 1984, p.210).

After the war, the communists took over a poor and devastated land, divided by culture, religion, and national feelings. They feared that the Orthodox Church could become the soul and the promoter of Serbian nationalism, and - more importantly - that the Roman Catholic Church could take leadership in Croatian nationalism.

Since Tito's death in 1980, Yugoslavia has hit on hard times. The living standard has fallen more than fifty percent. The foreign debt is nineteen billion dollars. Tito had managed to give Yugoslavia a kind of unity by dictatorial methods, but, since Tito, Belgrade's authority has fallen, and the country's various ethnic groups - especially the Serbs and the Croatians - find themselves more divided than ever culturally and politically. The Communist Party itself has split along regional lines. Inflation has mounted to eighty percent annually. The average monthly wage comes to about one hundred dollars; a four person family in a city need double that just for food. And relations between the Catholic Church and the government have considerably worsened.

Since Tito, the anti-Catholicism of the government has become more repressive. It has sharply reacted to Cardinal Kuharich's attempts to justify the Croatian love and respect for the late Cardinal Stepinac. A parish priest in the archdiocese of Split objected to children coming to catechism wearing badges with the picture of Tito, and was sent to prison. Local authorities bull-dozed a Marian shrine, a Lourdes grotto, near Makarska on the Adriatic coast. Large religious assemblies are often impeded or simply not allowed. And, of course, the events at Medjugorje have greatly alarmed both the local authorities and those in Belgrade.

This helps to explain how the communist government might fear any Roman Catholic revival, like the present one centering on Medjugorje, as a step toward Croatian (including the Croatian speakers of Bosnia-Herzegovina) autonomy or at least relative independence. The Belgrade government fears Croatian nationalism as much perhaps as Croatian religion. Historically, they have gone together.

In fact, Medjugorje contributes strongly to the overall Yugoslavian religious revival that so concerns Yugoslavian authorities. The proportion of young people that describe themselves as religious has jumped from one third in 1964 to over half in 1985. A recent poll of young people, both communist and non-communist, reveals that Mother Teresa of Calcutta stands first as the most popular figure; Lenin came in last, with only five per cent of the votes.

Yugoslavian communists understand the rise in religion among youth only in political terms; they identify it with a rise in nationalism. In particular, they see the present revival among Croatians in terms of Croatian nationalism; they see it as political because they understand religion as a rival ideology.

There is, in fact, a political aspect to Church life in the diocese of Mostar, where Medjugorje is located. This ecclesiastical political complication does not interest the communist authorities. But is has greatly muddied the religious waters, confusing Catholics. It is called "the Herzegovina case."

The Herzegovina case

In 1942, Rome appointed a diocesan priest as Bishop of Mostar, a diocese which had been governed for centuries by Franciscan bishops. The new bishop asked the Holy See to transfer some of the parishes of the diocese from the Franciscans to his diocesan clergy. Finally, in 1967 and even more forcefully and with greater precision in 1975, the Holy See ordered the Franciscans to turn over seven parishes to the bishop for his diocesan priests. The Franciscans claimed that this would do serious spiritual harm to the people of those parishes.

In 1976 Rome abolished the Franciscan provincial government in Herzegovina and put the Franciscans there directly under the Franciscan General Superior in Rome. Father John Vaughn, an American elected General in 1979, and recently re-elected for another six-year term, tried to find a solution to the problem by appointing a strong and able Croatian as his delegate for the government of the Herzegovinian Franciscans. The seven parishes, however, after over forty years, remain Franciscan.

In 1980, Bishop Pavao Zanic succeeded the retired Bishop of Mostar, and immediately divided the one parish of Mostar into two parishes, creating out of most of the former parish a new cathedral parish. He personally announced his plan to the people, saying that the division of the parish had been decided in agreement with the Franciscan superiors. One of the latter, who was also the pastor of the parish concerned, immediately rose to his feet to deny that there had been any such agreement. Within days, Bishop Zanic had this priest removed from his parish and deprived of his priestly faculties. Many of the parishioners refused to have anything to do with the diocesan priests of the new parish and continued to seek out Franciscans for Mass, the sacraments, and spiritual counselling. And so some Franciscans, having decided in conscience, began to say Mass and administer the sacraments to these people in chapels and private homes within the new parish boundaries.

In April 1981 Bishop Zanic attempted to put some order into the situation by expelling from his diocese two of these priests who had disobeyed him, Fathers Ivan Prusina and Ivica Vego. In 1982 the Franciscan Order expelled them and suspended them from all priestly ministry. They now reside in the Franciscan monastery in Mostar, together with their Provincial Superior who, of course, is not at all autonomous but remains directly under the delegate in Rome of the Franciscan General. They have applied to Rome for reinstatement in the Franciscan Order, having been expelled without a hearing of their defense.

Father Faricy met and talked with the two men. They are quite young, even boyish. They impressed him with their simplicity and traditional piety. They seem to have no rancor or bitterness toward anyone.

The Bishop of Mostar

Into this troubled and divided diocese came the blessed Virgin Mary in June of 1981. She could not have chosen a more difficult situation. On July 25 of the same year, Bishop Zanic spoke about the apparitions to the parish congregation in the church of St. James at Medjugorje as he preached on their patronal feast. "I am profoundly convinced," he said in a recorded homily, "that the children are not lying." In other statements, both private and public, he appeared quite favorable to the Medjugorje apparitions.

The bishop's attitude changed, however. Vicka, Mirjana and Jakov claimed that our Lady had told them, in answer to their questions about the two young expelled priests, that the bishop had acted hastily. Bishop Zanic told Father Faricy in a conversation a few years ago that he knows with certainty that the blessed Virgin would not criticize the local bishop.

Father Tomislav writes concerning this, "Monseigneur the bishop concerns himself always and exclusively with the message given by Vicka. Now this girl is choleric and has a brusque and sometimes aggressive style. Therefore the message that she gave had certainly her patina ... I asked the same question of the two visionaries Vicka and Mirjana. Both gave an answer with the same content but with differing expressions. While Vicka expressed the message in a choleric way, attacking the bishop a little, Mirjana gave the same message sweetly. These are Mirjana's exact words: "Our Mother (our Lady) said to the bishop that he was a little precipitate in his decision, that he must think again and listen again to both sides. She begged him to be just and patient. She, the dear Mother, thinks that her two servants have not done anything bad." (Letter of Tomislav Vlasic, O.F.M. to Rev. V. De Bernardi, S.J., 3 August, 1984)

Bishop Zanic has a strong devotion to our Lady, and he has visited all the principal Marian shrines in Europe. But he does not believe in the authenticity of the Medjugorje apparitions. He has stated that he has not yet made his final judgement. "If I am wrong," he has said, "I am willing to retract everything and go do penance at Medjugorje."

A letter from the Bishop of Mostar to the secretary of the Italian Conference of Bishops, dated 21 January 1984, in which he assures the Italian bishops that the alleged apparitions at Medjugorje "are strictly tied from their beginnings to the Herzegovina case which has gone on for decades, but especially since 1967," goes on to say that, after he learned that certain "messages from our Lady" protected "the two friars expelled from the order and admonished the local bishop", he had serious reservations about the events at Medjugorje.

A quite long document (twenty-three pages) entitled "The Present Position, Not Official, of the Episcopal

Curia of Mostar regarding the Events at Medjugorje" with the date of 30 October 1984, in Italian, was sent by Bishop Zanic to many persons, including Father Faricy. The document laments "the pilgrimages to Medjugorje," and expresses "the fear that all this may bring shame to the Church and to the Catholic faith, and great illusion to pious souls." The document goes on to say that many factors prompt the bishop to speak out, even though he does so unofficially; in particular, he refers to "articles, bulletins, pamphlets, books written by well-known but irresponsible theologians, television programs, videocassettes, superficial journalism, exalted charismatics."

At first, he writes, the bishop had thought that perhaps our Lady had come to resolve the Herzegovina case, and "to bring the disobedient (Franciscans) to obedience and to love of the Church." But later, at the end of the summer of 1981, he began to doubt seriously the authenticity of the apparitions.

Bishop Zanic accuses Father Tomislav Vlasic, at one time pastor of Saint James' parish and spiritual director of the young people who see and speak with our Lady, of making up the messages himself, and of asking in them for conversion, prayer, and penance so that they will appear more authentic.

The document's conclusion speaks of Bishop Zanic's "moral certainty that in the events of Medjugorje one finds a case of collective hallucination" that "was skilfully exploited by a group of Franciscans." He continues, accusing Father Tomislav of perjury and of being a "hoaxer and a charismatic magician." He states as the motive of this group of Franciscans: to show that the bishop and the legitimate superiors of the Franciscan Order "are in error regarding the famous question of the division of the parishes." "The presumed seers," he writes, "are unwitting instruments in a game much greater than they."

The bishop concludes by accusing Father René Laurentin, the distinguished mariologist, of writing and speaking about Medjugorje in order to gain "easy, fast money." And he deplores the fact that the emotional excitement about Medjugorje will "sooner or later·burst like a soap bubble, discrediting the authority of the Church" and of those in positions of responsibility "who have accredited the authenticity of the apparitions without waiting for official judgement."

In the same document, Bishop Zanic writes that he has tried to keep the Holy See informed about all the events of Medjugorje, and that, at the time of the document, he had spoken twice to the Pope. Pope John Paul, he writes, urged him to "proceed with great caution." On another visit to Rome, Bishop Zanic was cautioned not to hurry in pronouncing judgement on the Medjugorje events.

In a letter of 29 January 1985, the bishop complains to the Vatican Secretariat of State and to the Council of Public Affairs about the activities of Father Laurentin and of Archbishop Frane Franic of Split regarding their public approval of the Medjugorje apparitions.

On 25 March 1985, the Bishop of Mostar wrote a letter to the pastor of Saint James' parish, Father Tomislav Pervan, O.F.M. He writes that he has come "to a conclusion that is certain that the events of Medjugorje are not really about appearances of our Lady." He refers to a meeting with Father Pervan in the fall of 1984 in which the bishop "requested that the events of Medjugorje 'be brought down to earth and slowly extinguished.'" He complains that things have nonetheless remained the same.

And he gives several orders. First, that the "visionaries" do not appear publicly in the church and the "visions" do not take place in the church. Second, that the new statue of our Lady (a statue painted to resemble the descriptions given of our Lady in the appearances) "be removed without comment one night from in front of the altar and the old one is to be replaced." Third, that preaching about the apparitions is to stop, no messages are to be revealed, any pious practices that have developed out of the "apparitions" and the message are to be discontinued, and the sale of all souvenirs and literature propagating the "apparitions" must be discontinued in the parish. The letter forbids certain priests, including Father Tomislav

Vlasic, from preaching and celebrating Mass in the parish. Finally, it orders the pastor to collect everything the "visionaries" have written concerning the apparitions and to turn it over to him.

We visited Medjugorje shortly after this letter arrived, and we witnessed the obedience of the pastor and of the other parish priests. In fact, the young people no longer wait for our Lady to appear in the small side room in the church. As of this writing, she appears to them in the rectory. The pastor has removed the statue. And the Franciscans have followed the other orders.

On 11 January 1982, the Bishop of Mostar named a four-person commission to collect and examine data regarding the facts of Medjugorje. Early in 1984 the bishop expanded this commission to twenty persons. The enlarged investigating commission now includes not only priests from the Mostar diocese, but also theologians from Croatia and Slovenia, and representatives of the medical sciences. It met for the first time for two days in March 1984, and again in May. It requested that the organization of pilgrimages to Medjugorje be discouraged. In fact, in October 1984, and again in April 1985, the Bishops' Conference of Yugoslavia announced that "Official pilgrimages to Medjugorje should not be organized" until the apparitions are officially recognized by the Church, and that the bishops are following the events at Medjugorje with the attention they require.

Archbishop Franic

Archbishop Frane Franic, Archbishop of Split, is the President of the Yugoslavian Bishops' Conference's Committee for the Doctrine of the Faith. Matters such as the authenticity of apparitions commonly come under the supervision of such a committee of a national bishops' conference. Archbishop Franic, then, when he writes in a letter answering a question about the forbidding of the organization of pilgrimages, speaks with great authority:

> In reference to the document of the Yugoslavian Bishops' Conference, I hold that one must underline the word "official" pilgrimages. This means pilgrim-

ages organized by the dioceses and that have with them as official guides, bishops and cardinals. These pilgrimages imply an official profession of faith that would be premature at the present state of things. There remain permitted pilgrimages of devotion that express an experience of faith and prayer of pilgrims, including pilgrimages accompanied by priests, pilgrims themselves, acting as spiritual guides. (Letter of 12 November 1984 to Rev. M. Rastrelli, S.J., of Naples, Italy.)

In a letter to the same person, written two days later, Archbishop Franic says:

> Speaking globally, I have no doubt whatever about the supernatural character of the religious phenomena of Medjugorje. God with his spirit is present in that place. We must avoid the fanaticism of an overly literal interpretation of the messages and the facts; and we must also avoid every merely humanistic rationalism according to which there would by at Medjugorje no supernatural messages or facts, and everything would be explained by the pride of the children and the material interests of the Franciscans, and even by the devil one would see behind the children's pride and the avarice of the Franciscans .....
>
> ... I write this letter with full consciousness of the responsibility of my post as President of the Yugoslavian Bishops' Conference's Committee for the Doctrine of the Faith.

Archbishop Franic has repeated these views in an interview given to *Glas Koncila*, the Catholic newspaper published in Zagreb, published in the 16 December 1984 issue. In that interview he adds that ordinary pilgrimages should not be discouraged. The bishops' conference prohibits pilgrimages *officially* organized and officially led by bishops because the conference does not want to prejudge the results of the investigating commission. "It would be absurd," he said, "to order that pilgrimages be stopped before the diocesan commission establishes whether these apparitions are from God ..." In the same interview, the archbishop advises the Franciscans "to give those seven blessed parishes to the bishop; surely our Lady would be happy ..." He adds, "But those are human weaknesses ... In the investigation, human imperfections must be prescinded from, and the real substance of these revelations determined."

> People make mistakes. Young people remain young people; outside of a vision they could say things that don't stand up, they could lie, they could be disobedient, they could be distracted at prayer .... A scientific exegesis should be applied there. I myself have observed the situation, and I have talked with experts .... All of them agreed that these phenomena should be investigated seriously and not with the presupposition that they are a hallucination .... If the children were to hallucinate for three years and remain healthy, that would be a miracle in itself.

Father Slavko Barbaric interviewed Archbishop Franic in mid-December 1984. This interview took place in a car driving the archbishop back to Split from Medjugorje, where he had for the first time been present in the same room with the young people when our Lady appeared to them. In the interview, Archbishop Franic says that he holds the apparitions of our Lady and the whole Herzegovina case to be two quite separate questions. The matter of the authenticity of the apparitions should not be mixed up with the division of the parishes or with the expulsion of the two young Franciscans.

Archbishop Franic visited Vicka, Marija, Jakov, and Ivan in their homes. All four greatly impressed him. He also visited Jelena and Marijana, and they impressed him even more.

"Our Lady is appearing in Medjugorje," the archbishop said. "That is my conviction." He understands Medjugorge as in a direct line with Lourdes and Fatima. "The Holy Spirit is bringing about the renewal of the Church through Mary," he said in the interview.

The investigating commission

Bishop Pavao Zanic is the president of the diocesan investigating commission, named by him in 1982, and expanded from four members to twenty in 1984. It has issued two official reports on its work. The first, two brief pages put together at the end of a meeting of the commission held in the diocesan offices in late March 1984, relates that

> ... The members of the commission have visited Medjugorje during the Mass and the evening devotions on 23 March.
>
> The reason that the commission has not met more often before now lies in the fact that it was waiting for some qualitatively new development regarding the seers (for example, the visions coming to an end, or some other new factor regarding the apparitions). Another reason is the suggestion made by the Holy See to the local bishop not to hurry the investigation and his judgement as to the events because experience in similar situations elsewhere has shown time to be a good counselor for a prudent discernment.

The commission goes on to request that no further material on Medjugorje be published until a judgement by competent authority has been promulgated, or at least, if something be published that it be written reponsibly and objectively. The commission states its disapproval of pilgrimages to Medjugorje. It requests that the priests and the seers of Medjugorje make no public statements as to the content of the apparitions, and that the seers not be set apart from the rest of the congregation in the church. In the report, the commission makes no judgement on the authenticity of the apparitions.

Although Father Faricy received the first commission report in the mail shortly after its meeting in 1984, he has not received a report of the second meeting of the commission held again in the bishop's offices in Mostar, 7 and 8 March 1985. We have found no mention of this report in the press outside of Yugoslavia, but it was published in the Croatian Catholic paper *Glas Koncila* on 24 March 1985.

The report states simply what the commission discussed at its meeting: the published opposition to its views on the part of some Croatian bishops; published criticism of the composition of the commission; fasting, penance, and conversion in the messages of Medjugorje; theological difficulties; disciplinary problems in the parish and in particular the problem of the two expelled Franciscans who remain in Mostar. The commission also heard a report on the eschatological threats of the messages, that is: the power of Satan over the world, the threat of imminent destruction, secret signs that will end the time of any possible conversion. Two psychologists of the commission reported on their psychological testing of the seers and of some of the Franciscans in the parish. The commission also discussed the charismatic renewal elements that it has ascertained to have infiltrated into certain prayer groups at Medjugorje.

The report is not entirely clear in some respects, and it makes no definite judgement on the events in question. In fact, like the first report, it gives the impression that considerable time will elapse before the commission makes a final judgement.

The commission met again on 30 and 31 May 1985. This time, it finally began seriously to interview persons closely connected with the events at Medjugorje. It conducted an official interview with Father Jozo Zovko, O.F.M., the Medjugorje pastor at the time of the first apparitions in 1981. However, it has not even really begun to examine the young people and to look into the numerous reported healings.

Father Faricy writes: "I visited Bishop Zanic in February 1985, before the two commission meetings, and we talked about the commission. I asked what would happen if the commission found itself divided in opinion on Medjugorje and so unable to arrive at a unanimous conclusion. The bishop replied that the judgement of events at Medjugorje would not come from the commission but from him, and that he had already quite made up his mind that the blessed Virgin Mary was certainly not appearing at Medjugorje."

The Holy See

How does Rome view Medjugorje? We cannot expect an

official judgement from the Holy See until the final report of the Mostar investigating commission. And that, apparently, is a very long way off.

It appears quite unlikely, however, that either the Bishops' Conference of Yugoslavia or the Holy See will permit Bishop Zanic to make any official statement, at least before the apparitions have finished. And it seems entirely possible that either the Bishops' Conference or the Vatican will take over the official investigation into the matter of Medjugorje, if not soon, then probably after the end of the apparitions. Father Faricy has been assured by the Roman Congregation for the Doctrine of the Faith, headed by Cardinal Ratzinger, that they are following events in Medjugorje. Cardinal Ratzinger's congregation looks into matters of the Catholic faith; alleged apparitions of our Lady fall under its surveillance. At present, they have sent no representatives to Medjugorje to investigate matters; they await the final judgement of the Mostar commission.

The Congregation for the Doctrine of the Faith has close links with many well known Catholic theologians. It has surely listened to those who have expressed their views on Medjugorje. Father René Laurentine of France, the foremost Catholic expert on Marian apparitions, has written and spoken enthusiastically about Medjugorje; he is convinced of the authenticity of the apparitions. Father Michael Carroll of Ireland, the best known Mariologist in Ireland and England, has written several articles in favor of the authenticity of the Medjugorje events. Father Hans Urs von Balthazar of Switzerland, recognized as one of the two or three most outstanding Catholic theologians, has expressed a firm belief in the authenticity of our Lady's appearances at Medjugorje and appalled outrage at some of Bishop Zanic's stated views. As far as we know, no reputable Catholic theologian has put in writing any opinion unfavorable to Medjugorje, or even any serious reserves. In fact, all whom we have read are quite favourable. Cardinal Ratzinger, a front-rank theologian himself, is aware of this theological consensus. In an interview, he said that "... we can certainly not stop God from speaking in our times, even through simple persons and extraordinary signs that reveal the inadequacy of a culture like ours, rotten with rationalism" (*Pagine Aperte*, 1/85, 11).

Will Rome intervene? Will the Bishop of Mostar speak out officially condemning Medjugorje? What will happen? What official action will the Church take? At least for some time, probably none.

In the meantime, Medjugorje suffers. Necessarily, it seems. In the whole history of Christianity, since Mary said "Yes" to God at the Annunciation, God has revealed himself to us in and through suffering - in his own suffering on the cross, in the suffering of his martyrs right up to today, and in the suffering of his Church. The cross on Mount Krizevac, standing over Medjugorje, reminds us that there is no epiphany without the cross.

Church approval of the apparitions at Medjugorje

What would such approval mean? When and how might it take place? Church approval of Marian apparitions can take various forms. For example, the visits of Pope Paul VI and Pope John Paul II to Fatima indicate their approval of the Fatima apparitions. By "Church approval" here, however, we do not mean such instances; we mean formal Church approval.

Formal Church approval means this as a minimum: Church authority speaks out officially stating that the apparitions or the revelations in question contain nothing contrary to Catholic faith or morals. This does not of course mean that the fact of the apparitions is necessarily approved, although it can be. Nor does it mean that the Church necessarily approves the content of the messages. And it does not mean that Catholics have to believe in such apparitions, such as those at Lourdes or at Fatima. It means, simply, that the messages contain nothing contrary to faith or morals.

Church approval can come from different levels of ecclesiastical authority. For example, the local bishop of Medjugorje, the Bishop of Mostar, could officially state that the Medjugorje messages contain nothing against faith or morals. Or the assembled bishops of Croatia or of all of Yugoslavia could do the same. Or the Holy See could give such approval. Normally, the statement of approval should come from the local authority, from the Bishop of Mostar or from an official assembly of bishops of the Croatian Republic or of the Yugoslavian nation.

In fact, in the past, statements of approval have come from the local bishop rather than from the Holy See. The Roman authorities, for the most part, leave such decisions to the bishop of the diocese. Before the Council of Trent, in the sixteenth century, such formalities as Church approval of apparitions hardly existed. The apparitions of Our Lady of Guadalupe in 1531, for instance, were the object of several inquiries that had no special result. Nevertheless, Our Lady of Guadalupe was proclaimed Patroness of Mexico City in 1737, of all of "New Spain" in 1756, of Latin America in 1910, and of the Philippines in 1935; and both Pius XII and John XXIII spoke approvingly of the apparitions.

The great modern series of well-known apparitions, those with a universal public effect on the life of the Church, began with the Miraculous Medal apparitions of our Lady to Saint Catherine Labouré in the Rue du Bac convent chapel in Paris in 1830. There followed the apparitions of La Salette (1846), Lourdes (1858), Pontmain in France (1871), Pellevoisin (1876), Knock in Ireland (1879); Fatima (1917), and Beauraing and Banneux, both in Belgium (1932 and 1933). Approval varied according to the case. The Pontmain apparitions have never been officially approved, although a shrine has been erected there. Four years after the Lourdes apparitions to fourteen-year-old Bernadette Soubirous at the grotto of Massabielle, Bishop Laurence of Tarbes confirmed the apparitions and approved public devotion to Our Lady of Lourdes. The Bishop of Leiria in Portugal approved the Fatima apparitions and authorized devotion to Our Lady of Fatima in 1930, after a seven-year canonical investigation and thirteen years after the fact. More recently, at Akita, in northern Japan, Bishop Jean Ito Shojiro in 1982 officially approved public devotion to "Our Lady of Akita" after an investigation into the case of a statue of Mary that wept real tears on more than one hundred occasions in the years 1975 to 1981. The Bishop of Akita stated: "This is a matter of only private revelation; however, the Church gives great importance to private revelations, because they can help us to attain salvation."

Given the violent opposition of the communist authorities to the Medjugorje apparitions, one does not see how the local bishop could safely give them even minimal approval. Surely, no approval will come from any ecclesiastical authority until the apparitions have finished. And, even then, such approval may have to come from the Yugoslavian Bishops' Conference or from the Holy See.

A recent event, however, points to forthcoming approval at some time in the future. Mark Miravalle, an American layman, defended his doctoral thesis on the Medjugorje message on 31 May 1985, at the Pontifical University of Saint Thomas Aquinas in Rome. The doctoral dissertation treats precisely of the content of the Medjugorje messages up to March 1985. Miravalle relates the principal messages, analyzes them thematically, and evaluates them in the light of Scripture and in the light of the Second Vatican Council documents and of post-conciliar documents from the Holy See. He finds a remarkable correlation between Medjugorje and Church teaching. And he finds nothing contrary to Catholic faith and morals. The examining board, made up of three Roman theologians of the Dominican Order, including the eminent theologian Jordan Aumann, O.P., gave the defense a nearly perfect mark. That such a thesis, precisely on the content of the Medjugorje messages, has been written, defended, and highly approved at a Roman pontifical university has major significance.

It is permissible now to believe in the authenticity of the apparitions of Medjugorje and to state such belief publicly? Yes, of course. We do so in this book. Church approval of whatever kind is not needed for belief in such apparitions, even for publicly professed belief in them.

6. Messages for Christian Life

From all that our Lady, Queen of Peace, is saying at Medjugorje, especially in the messages she is giving for the people of the parish, a pattern begins to emerge. It is a program for Christian living. It looks like this:

On waking in the morning: pray.
Mary said: I want you to draw your life from prayer. Each morning on waking, pray: (at least say five "Our Father"s, five "Hail Mary"s and five "Glory be"s, with a sixth for the Holy Father the Pope). Then say the Creed, and a prayer to the Holy Spirit. And if it is possible it would be good to say the rosary. (to Jelena, 27 January 1984)

Scripture
Pray a reasonable time in the morning; read a passage of scripture and plant the divine word in your heart, and try to live it during the day especially in moments of trial. So you will be stronger than evil. (to Jelena, 19 April 1984)

I ask you to read the Bible in your homes every day, and let it be in a visible place there so that it always encourages you to read and pray.
(to Marija, 18 October 1984)

At the very first Thursday of the parish meetings our Lady gave the people a scripture passage. She said:

Every Thursday read anew before the Blessed Sacrament, or if it is not possible to come to church, do it with the family - read again the passage from the Gospel of Matthew 6:24-34 (to Jelena, 1 March 1984)

Before beginning work
Always pray before your work and end your work with prayer. If you do that, God will bless you and your work. These days you have been praying too little and working too much. In prayer you will find rest. (to Marija, 5 July 1984).

Mass
I want the holy Mass to be the gift of the day for you. Go to it, long for it to begin, because Jesus himself gives himself to you during the Mass. So live for this moment when you are purified. Pray much that the Holy Spirit will renew your parish. If people assist at Mass in a half-hearted fashion, they return home with cold, empty hearts. (to Jelena, 30 March 1984).

Dear children, I am calling you to more attentive prayer and participation in the Mass. I wish your Mass to be an experience of God. (to Marija, 16 May 1985).

Encourage the very young to pray and to go to holy Mass. (to Jelena, 7 March 1985)

Weekly fast, and the rosary
Fast strictly on Wednesday and Friday. Say at least one rosary: joyful, sorrowful and glorious mysteries.
(to Ivan, 14 August, 1984)

I beg the families of the parish to pray the family rosary.
(to Marija, 27 September 1984)

Family prayer
Today I call you to a renewal of family prayer in your homes. Let prayer take the first place in your families.
(to Marija, 1 November 1984)

Let all the prayers you say in your homes in the evening be for the conversion of sinners, because the world is in great sin. Pray the rosary every evening.
(to Jakov, 8 October 1984)

Evening
Pray also in the evening when you have finished your day. Sit down in your room and say to Jesus, "Thank you." If in the evening you fall asleep in peace and praying, in the morning you will wake up thinking of Jesus, and you will be able to ask him for peace. But if you fall asleep distracted, in the morning you will be hazy, and you will

forget even to pray. (to Jelena, 30 October 1983)

Almost always our Lady ends her message with the words, "Thank you for your response to my call."

BASICS AND DEVELOPMENT

During recent months our Lady has developed the themes of this basic way of Christian living. She has been leading the parish deeper into prayer, love, conversion and peace.

The parish is to be a model for all others

Dear children, I beg *all of you* especially those from this parish, to live my messages and tell them to whomever you meet. (to Marija, 16 August 1984)

Dear children, in your life you have all experienced light and darkness. God gives to each person knowledge of good and evil. I am calling you to the light, which you have to carry to all people who are in darkness. From day to day, people who are in darkness come to your homes. Give them, dear children, the light.
(to Marija, 14 March 1985)

Love is the chief message to the parish, and is the chief characteristic of the people there. Love comes from prayer, and leads to peace. It begins at home, in the family:

> Without love you will attain nothing. Therefore, first of all start loving your family, everyone in the parish, and then you will be able to love and accept all those who are coming here. Let this be the week of learning to love. (to Marija, 13 December 1984)

In November she had told them:

> Dear children, you do not know how to love, and you do not know how to listen with love to the words I am giving you. Be aware, my beloved, that I am your Mother, and that I have come to the earth to teach you how to listen out of love, how to pray out of love, and

> not out of compulsion because of the cross you are carrying. Through the cross God is being glorified in every person. (to Marija, 29 November 1984).

And on 6 June 1985, to Marija:

> Dear children, these days, people will be coming to the parish from all nations; so I am calling on you to love. Love first of all your own household, and then you will be able to love all who are coming.

In February, our Lady's message to the parish had been:

> With love you will achieve everything, and even what you think is impossible. God wants this parish to belong to him completely. And I want that too!
>
> (February 28, 1985 to Marija)

To Jelena, on 18 January 1984 Mary said:

> Pray! I wish to carve in each heart the sign of love. If you love every person you have peace in yourself. If you are at peace with everyone, peace reigns.

Jelena, now thirteen years old, used to see our Lady in an interior way but in 1985 began seeing her in exterior visions. Jelena exclaimed, "You are so beautiful!" Mary responded, "I am beautiful because I love. If you want to be beautiful - love."

In March 1985 our Lady's call to the parish became more urgent. She reiterated her predilection for the Medjugorje parish, and urgently asked the people to accept and live her messages. She said:

> Dear Children, I want to give you the messages, and therefore today also I call you to accept and to live my messages. Dear children, I love you, and in a special way I have chosen this parish which is more dear to me that others where I have gladly been when the Almighty sent me. Therefore I call to you: accept me, dear children, for your well-being. Follow the messages. Thank you for your response to my call.
>
> (to Marija, 21 March 1985).

The response of the people of Medjugorje will probably

be repeated by all of us who hear the messages - some will respond and produce a hundred-fold, some less, and some no fruit. Not all were immediately converted.

> Dear Children, this evening I ask you to stop slandering, and pray for the unity of the parish. For my Son and I have a special plan for this parish.
>
> (to Marija, 12 April 1984).

Some began well but did not persevere. On Thursday, 26 April 1984, no message was given. Marija asked our Lady on 30 April: "Dear Lady, why did you not give me the message for the parish on Thursday?" Our Lady replied,

> Even though I had a special message for the parish to awaken the faith of every believer, I do not wish to force anyone to anything they don't feel or don't want. Only a small number have accepted the messages on Thursdays. At the beginning there were more, but now it seems as if it has become something ordinary to them. And some have been asking recently for the message only out of curiosity and not out of faith and devotion to my Son and me.

Part of the reason is excessive concern with the necessary things of this world:

> In Medjugorje many people are intent on materialism from which they draw some profit, but they forget the one and only good. (to Jelena, 18 November 1983 - which was before the parish meetings began).

Each Thursday the parishioners read at our Lady's request the gospel passages from Matthew 6:24-34: "...no man can serve two masters ... do not worry about your livelihood ... your heavenly Father knows ..."

Mirjana, whose visions ceased on 25 December 1982, except for her birthday each year, reported on 18 March 1985 that our Lady "expressed her sorrow over the existence of so much greed in the world, including the greed here in Medjugorje. She said:

> Those who want to take everything away from those who come here (to pay their respects to her) should watch out, but blessed are the ones from whom they are taking.

An incomplete response saddens the Mother of God:

Dear children, today I would like to tell you that your prayers delight me, but there are those in the parish who do not pray and my heart is sad.

(to Marija, 4 October 1984)

Dear children, today I want to thank you for all your sacrifices; especially I thank those who have become dear to my heart and come here gladly. There are many parishioners who are not listening to the messages. But because of those who are in a special way close to my heart, because of them, I give messages to the parish. And I will continue giving them, for I love you and wish you to spread them by your hearts.

(to Marija, 10 January 1985)

In love she spoke severely to the parish and to all of us to whom her words apply:

Dear children, from day to day I have been appealing to you for renewal and prayer in the parish. But you are not accepting. Today I am appealing to you for the last time. This is the season of Lent, and you as a parish, in Lent, can be moved for the sake of love, to my call. If you do not do that, I do not wish to give you messages. God has permitted me.

(to Marija, 21 February 1985)

And on 9 May, 1985

Dear children, you do not know how many graces God is giving you. These days when the Holy Spirit is working in a special way, you do not want to advance. Your hearts are turned towards earthly things, and you are occupied by them. Turn your hearts to prayer and ask that the Holy Spirit be poured upon you.

Prayer

The most frequent message of our Lady at Medjugorje is "Pray!" She has explained,

When I say 'Pray, pray, pray', I don't mean only increase the hours of prayer, but increase the desire to pray and to be in contact with God, to be in a continuous prayerful state of mind. (reported by Father Tomislav Vlasic in an interview with Sister Lucy 26 June 1984)

But time given to prayer is so important that the Mother of God said to Jelena in May 1984,
I know that every family can pray four hours each day.
Jelena responded, "But if I tell this to the people, they may back out!"

You too don't understand - said our Lady - It is only one sixth of the day.

(interview with Father Vlasic, as above).

Many of the young people of the parish follow this call to prayer, but at the beginning they found the time long. Our Lady sent them a message:

You have begun to pray for three hours, but you look at your watches, preoccupied with your work. Be preoccupied with the one thing necessary, and let yourselves be guided by the Holy Spirit. Then your work will go well. Do not rush. Let your work be guided and you will see that everything will be accomplished well.

(to Jelena, 4 July 1983)

On 26 July, through Marija, our Lady sent a message to the youth of the parish:

Dear children, today also I would like to call you to persistent prayer and penance. Especially let the young people of this parish be more active in their prayer.

Mary has told us that prayer is the most effective way.

Pray, pray, pray! You will never get anything from talk, but only from prayer

(to Jelena, 27 October 1983)

Pray, pray. Prayer will give you everything. It is through prayer that you can obtain everything.

(to Jelena, 25 October 1983)

Dear children, today I want to call you: pray, pray, pray! In prayer you will come to know the greatest joy, and the way out of every situation that has no way out. Thank you for moving ahead in prayer. Every individual is dear to my heart. And I thank all of you who have rekindled prayer in your families.

(to Marija, 28 March 1985)

Why does our Lady ask for continuous prayer and for four hours a day from working families? She explained:

Dear children, I continually need your prayer. You wonder what all these prayers are for. Turn around, dear children, and you will see how much ground sin has gained in this world. Therefore pray that Jesus may conquer. (to Marija, 13 September 1984)

To Jelena she said,

Pray. Don't look for a reason why I am constantly asking you to pray. Intensify your personal prayer and let it spill over to others. (17 November 1983).

And again:

Dear children, the love of God has not flowed over the whole world; pray therefore.

On 2 August 1984 she said through Marija:

Dear children, today I am happy, and I thank you for your prayers. Pray more these days for the conversion of sinners.

What will be the fruit of this prayer?

Pray, pray. If you pray I shall watch over you and be with you. (to Jelena, 4 December 1983)

Before the novena for the feast of the Annunciation, Mary said to Jelena,

Pray and fast so that during the novena God will overwhelm you with his power. (17 March 1984)

To Jelena's prayer group our Lady said,

If you pray, a spring of life will flow from your hearts. (to Jelena, 21 October 1983)

The parish message on 15 November 1984 was:

I do not know what else to tell you because I love you and wish that in prayer you may come to know my love and the love of God.

Our Lady shows herself sensitive to our frailties in praying.

Dear children, I am begging you to pray more; and let your prayer be a sign of your surrender to God. Dear children, I know about your tiredness. But you don't know how to surrender yourselves to me. Surrender yourselves to me completely.

(to Marija, 13 June 1985)

The blessed Virgin gives two conditions for prayer: abandonment and peace. To Jelena's prayer group:

> I know that you pray a long time, but really hand yourselves over. (30 October 1983)

Father Tomislav, then the director of the children, gave his impression of our Lady's teaching on prayer: "The Madonna wants peace before prayer begins, she wants peace throughout the prayer - prayer finishes with peace, with an interior listening." (interview, 26 June 1984)

Trials, sin, suffering

The appearances of our Lady have brought suffering as well as joy to the boys and girls concerned, and to the parish whose way of life has been disrupted and put under pressure. Our Lady is aware of all this.

> Dear children, these days you have savoured the sweetness of God through renewal in your parish. Satan is working even more violently to take away the joy from each of you. Through prayer you can totally disarm him and ensure your happiness.
>
> (to Marija, 24 January 1985)
>
> In these days Satan is fighting deviously against this parish, and you, dear children, are asleep in prayer, and only some of you are going to Mass. Persevere in these days of temptation.
>
> (to Marija, 17 January 1985).

The battle against Satan is constant:

> Dear children, these days Satan is trying to thwart all my plans. Pray that his plan may not be fulfilled. I will pray my Son Jesus that he will give you the grace to experience his victory in Satan's temptations.
>
> (to Marija, 12 July 1984)
>
> Dear children, pray, because Satan is continually trying to thwart my plans. Pray with your heart and in prayer give yourselves up to Jesus.
>
> (11 August 1984)
>
> Dear children, I love this parish and with my mantle I protect it from every work of Satan. Pray that Satan flees from the parish and from every individual who comes to the parish. In that way you will be able to hear every call of God and answer it with your life.
>
> (to Marija, 11 July 1985)

On 25 June 1985 Mary said through Marija:

> I ask you, I ask everyone, to pray the rosary. With the rosary you will overcome all the troubles which Satan is trying to inflict on the Church. Let all priests pray the rosary. Give time to the rosary.

There was much suffering at Christmas:

> This Christmas Satan wanted in a special way to thwart God's plans. You, dear children, have discerned Satan even on Christmas day. But in your hearts God has conquered. Let your hearts be continually joyful.
>
> (to Marija, 27 December 1984)

New pressures on the parish in early 1985 brought this message from our Lady:

> Dear children, Satan is manifesting himself in this parish in a particular way these days. Pray, dear children, that God's plan is carried out, and that every work of Satan is turned to the glory of God. I have remained this long to help you in your great trials.
> (to Marija, 7 February 1985)

Sin

In May 1984 our Lady spoke about sin:

> Dear children, I have already told you that I have chosen you in a special way, the way you are. I, the Mother, love you all. And in any moment when it is difficult for you, don't be afraid. I love you even when you are far away from me and from my Son. I ask you not to allow my heart to cry with tears of blood because of the souls who are being lost in sin. Therefore, dear children, pray, pray, pray!
>
> (to Marija, 24 May 1984)

Temptation

Of temptation, Mary said,

> Do not be afraid of temptations. I am always with you. God is always watching over you. I sympathize with you in even the smallest temptation.
>
> (to Marija, 19 July 1984)

Suffering

Our Lady has spoken often of suffering and of using suffering for profit.

> Dear children, thank you for the offering of all your pains to God; even now he is testing you through the fruits you are reaping (heavy rain at harvest-time). Realize, dear children, that he loves you, and for that reason he tests you. Always present your burdens to God, and do not worry.
>
> (to Marija, 11 October 1984)

To Jelena our Lady said:

> I am your good Mother, and Jesus is your great Friend. Fear nothing in his presence, but give him your hearts. From the depth of your heart tell him your sufferings. In this way you will be revitalized in prayer, your heart set free and in peace without fear.
>
> (29 November 1983)

To Marija:

> Dear children, open your hearts to the Lord of all hearts. Give me all your feelings and all your problems. I wish to console you in all your temptations. I wish to fill you with the peace, joy and love of God.
>
> (20 June 1985)

Using human language, the blessed Virgin said to the parish:

> Dear children, this evening in a special way I am asking for your perseverance in trials. Ponder how the Almighty is still suffering because of your sins. So when sufferings come, offer them as your sacrifice to God.
>
> (to Marija, 29 March 1984)

Our Lady asked through Jelena that the people of the parish make some sacrifice each Thursday.

> On Thursdays let each one find their own way of fasting: the one who smokes should give up smoking, the one who drinks alcohol should not drink it; let each one give up some pleasure. Have these recommendations passed on to the parish. (1 March 1984)

The Holy Trinity.

Often Mary speaks of God our Father. On 31 January

1985 the parish message was:

Dear children, today I wish to tell you to open your hearts to God like flowers in spring, yearning for the sun. I am your Mother, and I always want you to be closer to the Father, and that he will give abundant gifts to your hearts. (to Marija)

Sometimes our Lady has been carrying the Child Jesus when she has appeared to the visionaries. During the Christmas season of 1984 she said through Jelena:

Children, pray. I repeat: pray! I say it to you again. Don't think that Jesus is going to show himself once again in the crib; but he is being reborn in your hearts. (8 January 1984)

And on 20 December 1984 through Marija she said:

Today I am asking you to do something practical for Jesus Christ. On the day of joy (Christmas Day) I wish that every family of the parish bring a flower as a sign of abandonment to Jesus. I wish that every member of the family has one flower next to the crib so that Jesus can come and see your devotion to him.

Our Lady recommends devotion to Jesus in the Blessed Sacrament, and she speaks often of his Heart and of his wounds.

This evening, dear children, in a special way I am grateful to you for being here. Continually adore the Most Holy Sacrament. I am always present when the faithful are in adoration. Special graces are then being received. (to Marija, 15 March 1984)

And on Thursday at the parish meeting, 5 April 1984, the message was:

Dear children, this evening I am especially asking you to venerate the Heart of my Son Jesus. Make atonement for the wounds inflicted on the Heart of my Son. That Heart has been offended with all sorts of sin. Thank you for coming this evening.

During Lent 1984, our Lady said:

Dear children, this evening I am asking you in a special way during this Lent to honor the wounds of my Son which he received from this parish. Unite with my prayers for this parish so that his sufferings may

> become bearable (to Marija, 22 March 1984)

The Holy Spirit

Our Lady speaks frequently of God the Holy Spirit. Before Pentecost 1984 she said:

> Tomorrow night pray for the Spirit of truth. Especially you from the parish. The spirit of truth is necessary for you in order to convey the messages just as I give them to you, not adding anything or taking anything away. Pray that the Holy Spirit may inspire you with the spirit of prayer, that you may pray more. I as your Mother say that you pray little. (to Marija, 9 June 1984)

To the two younger girls who see our Lady, apart from the six original visionaries, Mary spoke in March 1984. To Jelena on 5 March she said:

> Pray and fast. Ask the Holy Spirit to renew your souls, to renew the whole world.

To Marijana on 14 March:

> Pray and fast that the reign of God may come among you. Let my Son inflame you with his fire.

Through Marija, the message for the parish on 2 June 1984 was:

> Dear children, this evening I wish to say: in the days of this novena pray for the outpouring of the Holy Spirit upon all of your families and your parish. Pray, and you will not regret it. God will give you the gifts and you will glorify him for them till the end of your life.

In November of the same year our Lady said:

> Dear children, you are not aware of the messages which God is sending to you through me. He is giving you great graces, and you are not grasping them. Pray to the Holy Spirit for enlightenment. If you only knew the greatness of the graces God is giving you, you would pray without ceasing. (to Marija, 8 November 1984)

In the special difficulties of the spring of 1985, our Lady advised:

> Today I wish to tell everyone in the parish to pray in a special way for the enlightenment of the Holy Spirit. From today, God wants to try the parish in a special way in order that he may strengthen it in faith.
>
> (to Marija, 11 April 1985)

April 25 1985. Dear children, Today I want to tell you to begin to work in your hearts as you work in the fields. Work to change your hearts so that the Spririt of God may move in your hearts.

Fasting

All who fast on bread and water each Wednesday and Friday testify to the efficacy of the practice. The families of Medjugorje bake their own bread, and often fortify it by adding potatoes to the flour. The water normally drunk at meals is mineral water. The two words "fast" and "pray" are always linked in our Lady's messages, because each makes the other possible. In September 1984, for example, she said:

> Today I ask you to start fasting from your heart. There are many people who fast but only because everyone else is fasting. It has become a custom which no one wants to stop. I ask the parish to fast out of gratitude to God for allowing me to remain this long in this parish. Dear children, fast and pray with all your heart.
>
> (to Marija, 20 September 1984)

Confession

In the context of our Lady's message at Medjugorje, conversion means reconciliation with God and with others in the overall framework of the Church. Not surprisingly, Mary urges the Sacrament of Penance as a fundamental part of conversion. A good confession has its part in the beginnings of an authentic conversion, and regular, monthly, confession is a basic element in the ongoing conversion that the message of Medjugorje calls us to.

Mary talks about the need for confession already on the third day of the apparitions, 26 June 1981, when she appears to Marija walking home from the apparition to the group, and says,

> People must be reconciled with God and with one another. For this to happen, it is necessary to believe, to pray, to fast, and to go to confession.

She later speaks of the Sacrament of Reconciliation as a

medicine for the whole sick Church in the West, saying that whole areas of the Church would be healed if believers went to confession once a month.

The theme of reconciliation with God and among ourselves continues to be one of her main messages. To Jelena she said on 7 November 1983:

> Don't go to confession from habit and then stay the same after it. No, that is not good. Confession should give force to your faith. It should stir you and draw you nearer to Jesus. If confession does not mean much to you, you will be converted only with difficulty.

A message to the parish on the eve of the feast of the Annunciation, 1985, speaks of confession:

> Dear children, today I wish to call you to confession, even if you have had confession a few days ago. I wish you to experience my feast day within yourselves. You cannot unless you give yourselves to God completely. And so I am calling you to reconciliation with God.

Queen of Peace

When the apparitions first begain in the summer of 1981, Ivanka asked the Lady her name. "I am the blessed Virgin Mary" was the reply. When asked if she had another name, our Lady identified herself as "the Queen of Peace." She asked for 25 June to be dedicated to her under that title. Throughout the four years of the apparitions, Mary has not ceased emphasizing her reason for coming to earth. "I came because there are many good believers here. I want to be with you, to convert and to reconcile everyone." (26 June 1981)

During these four years our Lady has been teaching us the most effective way of working for world peace - that we each, individually, convert our lives, by faith, daily prayer, monthly confession and fasting. These four things are interlinked. Prayer and fasting, our Lady told the children, can avert wars and even natural disaster. We have both of these evils with us now as never before.

Mary gives us the way to individual and to world peace.

> Dear children, without prayer there is no peace. Therefore I say to you, pray at the foot of the cross for peace. (to Marija, 6 September 1984)

To Jelena, on 29 December 1983, she said:

> I want great peace, a great love to grow in you. Then pray.

And to Jelena on 29 October 1983:

> Prayer is the only way that leads to peace. If you pray and fast you will obtain all you ask.

7. Reflecting on the Message

Medjugorje as a fact, as a phenomenon, tells us something. The fact of Medjugorje is, already, in itself, a message. I do not mean to indicate by the word "fact" only what Marija, Jakov, Ivan, and Vicka perceive every day. I mean, rather, the whole fact that any of us can see if we go there, that all of us can know about through books, this one for instance, and newspapers. I mean the fact that a whole parish, including the pastor and all the other pastoral workers, firmly believes in the authenticity of Mary's guiding presence among them. The fact that this acceptance of her guidance, granted human failings, has through God's grace transformed the parish. The fact that thousands of pilgrims have met God in a new and more powerful way through Mary at Medjugorje. The fact that so many know, without reflecting theologically, without scientific investigation, without ability to adequately articulate what they know, that Mary is there, that Medjugorje is true, real. So many know through a kind of instinct of the faith, through a kind of mass guidance by the Holy Spirit, through that special providence that reveals the truth to the small and the simple and that hides it from those who think themselves wise.

What shape does that fact, the observable fact of the events at Medjugorje, have? We try to describe it here, in this book, by telling what we have seen and heard there. Here, in this chapter, I want to reflect on that overall fact, to reflect in faith, so as to express as well as I can what Medjugorje means. And I want to reflect on Mary's message, on what she says to us: peace, faith, conversion, fasting, prayer, confession - with a view to examining what that message means for each of us personally and for the Church as a totality.

Mary as Mother

Mary presents herself at Medjugorje as mother. She acts in an entirely motherly way with the young people to whom she comes every day. She is their spiritual director and their guide, their teacher of the spiritual life, and a model for them. And all this in a maternal manner. She acts as their mother in the order of grace, the mother of their spiritual lives, of their prayer and of all their Christian living.

Mary helps the young people to intercede for others - for those who ask them to intercede for them for special intentions, for the sick, for the conversion of the Bishop of Mostar, for the world, and especially for peace in the world. She prays with them, interceding with them. Just as our Lady acts as a mother of grace, a mother of their spiritual lives, so too she takes their prayers of intercession with her to the Lord.

That is, she exercises a "descending mediation" with respect to God's grace in their lives, and an "ascending mediation" regarding their prayers of intercession. In other words, she is a mother to them.

Mary's "mothering" of the young people finds its basis in the fact of her motherhood of Jesus. She is their mother because she is Jesus' mother. Vicka, Ivan, Marija, Jakov, Ivanka, and Mirjana all understand this quite well. So, for that matter, do Jelena and Marijana. Mary is the mother of the relationship between Jesus and each one of them because she is the mother of Jesus and, therefore, their mother too.

Mary present herself in the Medjugorje apparitions not only as the mother of the young persons to whom she appears, but also as the mother of everyone in the parish, and in fact as the mother of all of us. Mary shows herself at Medjugorje as the mother of the spiritual life, of the whole Christian life, for all of us, for each one of us personally. Her motherhood of all of us and of each of us personally is a strong element of the message implicit in the apparitions.

Sometimes in what she says our Lady refers explicitly to her motherhood of all of us. "I your Mother love you all," she tells the parish, and through the parish, all of us, in a Thursday message, 24 May 1984. She continues, "In difficult moments, do not be afraid; I love you even when you are far from me and my Son." Six months later, she tells the parish, "Be aware, my beloved ones, that I am your Mother, and that I come on earth to teach you to listen out of love, to pray out of love, and to carry your cross" (29 November 1984).

Motherhood is a permanent relation. Your mother is always your mother, even after the physical fact of her giving you life and birth has passed. So Mary remains forever Jesus' mother. Because Jesus has come to us in the first place through her, he come to us now through her. She acts, still, as the channel of Jesus' life in us. She is the mother of our lives with him, of our relationship with him, of grace in our lives. Our Lady told the parish of Medjugorje, "My Son Jesus Christ wants to bestow on you special graces through me" (17 May 1984). And, "I am his Mother, and I intercede for you with him" (undated, before 1984).

Mary "gave Life to the world." That is, she bore Jesus; she gave life to Life himself. That past historical fact provides the foundation for a real permanent relation of Mary to Jesus: she conceived and gave birth to him, and therefore she *is* his mother. (One's mother remains one's mother; the relation is permanent.) This means that Mary, because she was historically the point of contact between Jesus Christ and all humanity - i.e., she brought him into the world - remains that point of contact, because her maternal relation to Jesus is permanent (she is still his mother).

Jesus assumed human nature through Mary in order to by my Savior. My relation to him (as to my personal Savior) therefore passes through Mary. The relation of all humankind to Jesus comes to a point in Mary.

So my relation to Mary is this: she relates me to Jesus. Just as historically she related each person, and all persons, to Christ by conceiving and birthing him into human society, so too now - because she continues to be his mother - she "births him" to us, relates us to him. She births, mothers, the Christ-life in me, relating me to him. That is to say, she mothers the life of Jesus' Spirit in me. That life of the Holy Spirit is grace.

The useful image here is that of Mary at the foot of the

cross. Jesus says to his mother, "Woman, behold your son!" (John 19:26)

Mary gave Life to the world; she gives Life to me now; she mothers that new life (of grace) in me. Mary is my, our, mother in the order of grace.

Note that I am not related to Mary through Jesus, by being incorporated into his Body by baptism. That would put Mary above Christ. Just the opposite: Jesus is our one Mediator with the Father. He is unique as the one Mediator. That mediation, his mission to us, comes to us through Mary - as he did when he came to the world.

Mary is, as the Council says, mediatrix of the new life in us, but not at all in the same sense as Jesus is Mediator. Rather: in the sense that she is mother of our grace-life, mediatrix of grace. Mary is a "transparent" mediatrix, not at all getting between Jesus and us but rather facilitating the immediacy of our union with him.

That Mary is mediatrix of grace means that we can pray to her. The fact of descending mediation, from God through Mary to us, permits the possibility of ascending mediation. We can pray to Mary to pray for us. We can ask her to intercede. The New Testament image here is the wedding feast of Cana. We show to Mary our problems; she intercedes and says to us, as she said to the wine stewards, "Do whatever he tells you" (John 2:5).

This is the teaching of the Second Vatican Council's *Dogmatic Constitution on the Church,* Chapter Eight, the chapter dedicated entirely to our Lady. The preface of Chapter Eight quotes the only Pauline text referring to Mary: "When the fullness of time came, God sent his Son, born of a woman, ... that we might receive adoption as children" (Galatians 4:4-5). And then it immediately cites the Creed, "... and was incarnate by the Holy Spirit from the Virgin Mary." The preface then states its fundamental faith premise: "... the Virgin Mary received the Word of God in her heart and in her body, and gave Life to the world." The image that the Council gives us here, to help to concretize the fact of faith that Mary actively received God's Word and gave Life to the world, is that of the annunciation of the angel's message to

Mary, and her response (Luke 1:26-38).

From the fundamental fact that Mary is Jesus' mother, three important points follows: (a) Mary is closely and indissolubly united to Jesus; (b) as his mother, she is mother of all Christians; and (c) Christians then should acknowledge and honor her. These are sections 2,3, and 4 of the chapter.

The second section is heavily scriptural in showing Mary's closeness to Jesus. She is "the virgin who is to conceive," who ratifies the Father's choice by her consent. This consent means more than simply receiving; since Mary *consents* to receive, she participates - co-operates - in the work of salvation through free faith and obedience. So, she is the "Mother of the living," the mother of new life in us. Mary's union with Jesus can be seen in the visit to Elizabeth, in the presentation of Jesus in the temple, in Mary's later losing him and then finding him in the temple, and in her presence at the foot of the cross. That close union is further seen in the mysteries of Pentecost where Mary prayed with the others, of her assumption into heaven, and of her exaltation by Jesus as Queen of all.

The third section of Chapter Eight of *Lumen gentium* describes our Lady's relationship with the Church. The section begins by declaring the uniqueness of Jesus Christ as the one Mediator, and goes on to say that Mary's maternal role regarding us in no way diminishes the place of Jesus as Mediator of salvation - "rather, it shows its power." The text further states that, because Mary is Jesus' mother, "she is our mother in the order of grace."

The original *schema* stressed Mary as mediatrix of grace more than the final version does. Many fought the use of the term "mediatrix," conceding only when it became clear from the text that Mary's mediation is quite different from Christ's and in no way replaces it or takes anything away from it.

Motherhood is essentially a question of co-operating with God in his work of bringing new life into the world. Spiritual motherhood, then, means co-operating with God in his work of re-creation, in bringing the new life of the Spirit into the world. Mary co-operated with God in the Incarnation and in Jesus' whole work of our salvation. She continues to co-operate with God in the ongoing work of redemption by bringing new life into the world through her intercession. She is our mother in the order of grace.

The scriptural images that the Council offers us to help make more concrete its teaching on Mary's maternity are: the annunciation of the angel's message, and Mary's consent (Luke 1:26-38); and Mary at the foot of the cross (John 19:26-27). Mary's maternity in the order of grace began with her consent in faith at the message of the angel, a consent that she sustained standing beneath the cross. Besides being mother, Mary is a model. As the best, the most perfect of all the redeemed, she is a model for each of us.

Section four speaks of the reverence with which the Church honors the blessed Virgin Mary, carefully distinguishing that reverence from the worship offered to Jesus Christ, to the Father, and to the Holy Spirit. The last section recommends praying to Mary that she intercede for us and for the whole Church, since she is "the sign of sure hope and of consolation for the pilgrim people of God."

Vatican II's teaching on our Lady's maternity and on the fact that we can pray to her finds its continuation in the teachings of Popes Paul VI and John Paul II. Paul VI speaks of Mary as intercessor for the unity of Christians and for peace in the world, giving her the title, "Queen of Peace" *(Marialis cultus,* 1974, n. 5 and 33). John Paul II quotes Vatican II on Mary's maternity in the order of grace (*Dives in misericordia*, 1980, n. 9), teaches that Mary's motherhood of Jesus means that she has a special dignity and a unique role in our redemption (*Redemptor hominis*, 1979, n. 22). He refers to her ecumenical role, calling her "Mother of Unity" (Homily at Czestochowa, 6 June 1979), and calls her "Queen of Peace" (Homily at Guadalupe, 27 January 1979, n. 4)

Our Lady's message as prophecy

Catholic theology traditionally distinguishes between

"public revelation" and "private revelation." Public revelation ended with the death of the last apostle. It contains all that God has revealed to us in Jesus Christ. Public revelation contains both Scripture and tradition - that is, whatever has been divinely inspired and handed down to us from the time of Jesus and the apostles. We could put it this way: Jesus Christ risen contains in himself all that God wants to tell us; he is God's Word to us; having him, we have it all, even if we cannot fully understand not fully articulate it. Jesus Christ is the fulness of God's self-communication to us. Once the last apostolic witness to Jesus' resurrection disappeared from this world, revelation was, so to speak, "closed."

By exclusion, Catholic theology holds all other revelation to be "private revelation." For example, revelations made to a saint about the life of Jesus, or personal messages received by someone in prayer. Private revelation never adds anything to what we already have in Jesus, to public revelation. Private revelation reminds us, guides us, applies Christian truth to our situation, encourages us, corrects us, exhorts us. It sometimes reveals future events, perhaps conditionally, depending on prayer.

Even when private revelation has a certain public character, as in the cases of the Sacred Heart revelations to Margaret Mary Alacoque, the Miraculous Medal revelations to Catherine Labouré, or the messages of Fatima and Lourdes, we still call it "private revelation." In such cases, when the revelation is a message for a large group, for the whole Church, or for the world, then the revelation is properly prophetic.

Prophecy is a kind of revelation. It has a social role, and it is for all times. Thomas Aquinas says of prophecy that "in every period there have always been some who have the spirit of prophecy, not to set forth new teaching of the faith, but to give direction to human activities" (*Summa theologiae* II-II, 174, 6 *ad* 3). God can tell us what he wants to say to us through prophetic revelation, through prophecy.

The Medjugorje messages have this prophetic

character. They are "private revelation," but intended for the world, for all of us. They have a public character. And they are from God. We might say that the young persons whom our Lady visits daily receive prophecies, prophetic revelations, from her. Just as our Lady mediates God's grace, she has at Medjugorje - as at Lourdes and Fatima - a mediational role. She passes on the messages from God to the young people to whom she speaks.

Often, what our Lady says is only, or at least in the first instance, for a particular person or group; and, on Thursdays, for the parish. Here too we can speak of prophecy, of private revelation in a prophetic mode, mediated by Mary. When Jelena and Marijana receive messages from our Lady for the prayer group, whether the messages come before or during a prayer meeting, those messages are properly prophecies.

God speaks to us through Mary at Medjugorje. She speaks to us through young people who are, then, a prophetic voice for our times.

Like all prophetic messages, those of Medjugorje are subject to discernment. As in any prophecy, unauthentic elements can creep into the messages. Those who receive them mighty unconsciously distort them, or give false emphases, or add to or subtract from the messages. The discernment role belongs to the Church: to the Bishop of Mostar, to the Bishops' Conference of Yugoslavia, to the Holy See.

Peace, conversion, confession

Our Lady's message to the world is: peace, conversion, confession, faith, fasting, prayer. Mary's message is addressed to all of us, and to each of us. The messages for everyone have come through the regular "visionaries" who meet with our Lady every evening. Messages that our Lady gives through Jelena and Marijana are usually personal, or for particular groups such as the prayer group. Mary's messages to the parish, usually given through Marija on Thursday evenings, are not only for the parish but also for the whole world. "Dear children," she told the parish on 16 August 1984, "I beg all of you, especially those from this parish, to live my messages and to pass them on to those you meet; thank you for your response to my call."

The messages to the parish, then, are for all of us. The parish, guided by Mary, is to be a model for those outside the parish. And yet, not everyone in the parish accepts Mary's messages and tries to live them. Mary complains to the parish, "Today is the day when I give you a message for the parish, but not everyone in the parish accepts and lives the messages. This saddens me. I want you to listen to me, dear children, and to live my messages. Every family must have family prayer and Bible-reading" (14 February 1985). And again, the next week, Mary complains to the parish, "I have been appealing to you for prayer and renewal in the parish. But you do not accept my appeal. This is the season of Lent; and you, as a parish in the Lenten season, can move yourselves to accept my call out of love. If you do not, I do not wish to continue to give you the messages that God permits me to give you" (21 February 1985).

The messages, then, are not just words. They are words to live out, to put into practice. And so our Lady guides the parish, and all of us, not only by showing us what to do and by encouraging us to do it, but also by patient and understanding corrections and by calling us to greater conversion.

Our Lady's message is a message of peace. Peace comes from conversion. And conversion is brought about by faith, by fasting and other forms of penance, and by prayer.

A message of peace. The third day of the apparitions, 26 June 1981, our Lady appeared to Marija while she was walking home from the evening apparition. With tears in her eyes, Mary said, "Peace, peace, peace ... only peace. People must be reconciled with God and with one another. For this to happen, it is necessary to believe, to pray, to fast, and to go to confession. Go in God's peace."

That same first summer, a large number of people saw the word "MIR," Croatian for "peace," written in the sky over Mount Krizevac on 6 August. And at the end of August Mary identified herself as the "Queen of Peace."

Our Lady calls us to pray for peace in the world. "Christians have forgotten that they can prevent war and even natural calamities by prayer and fasting" (21 July 1982). To the parish, Mary said on 6 September 1984, "Dear children! Without prayer, there is no peace. Therefore I say to you, dear children, pray at the foot of the cross for peace."

Mary's message is one of peace, and primarily of peace of heart. When Father Tomislav Vlasic asked Mirjana why our Lady called herself "Queen of Peace," Mirjana answered, "Can't you see yourself that the situation in the world is horrible? Wars everywhere; the situation is tense. Peace is needed, just peace - peace in the soul first ... The main thing is peace of soul. If you have peace in your soul, then you have it around you." Peace comes "as a consequence of prayer, penance, and fasting" (10 January 1983).

The way to peace is through conversion. Mary gave the young people this message in an apparition on 20 April 1983, "The only word I want to say is about the conversion of the whole world. I want to say it to you so that you can say it to the whole world. I ask nothing but conversion. It is my desire. Be converted." She frequently calls for prayers for the conversion of sinners. Mary urges us to be converted and to pray for the conversion of the whole world, and she tells us to hurry, because there is little time left.

8. Apocalyptic Elements: Light and Darkness

The Marian apparitions at Medjugorje have strong apocalyptic elements, perhaps even more so than the apparitions at Fatima in 1917. The classic apocalyptic elements in the messages are: the ten secrets with their implied content of terrible future events, the frequent references to the devil, and the promised sign to appear at Medjugorje. Add to these the mysterious signs already witnessed at Medjugorje: strange lights, the sun changing color and moving strangely, visions had by large and small groups of people. And add the remarkable healings that take place there. Healings traditionally mark an apocalyptic mode - they demonstrate God's power to save.

The apocalyptic aspect permeates the events at Medjugorje and helps to account for part of Medjugorje's mystery and fascination. Let us look at the above apocalyptic elements one at a time. They make up part of the message. But first of all, what is apocalytic?

The nature of apocalyptic

Biblical examples of apocalyptic can be found in the books of Daniel, Ezekiel (Chapters 38 and 39), and Zechariah (Chapters 12-14), as well as in the New Testament Apocalypse (or Book of Revelation) and the apocalyptic statements of Jesus (espcially Mark, Chapter 13; Matthew, Chapters 24-25). Apocalyptic is both a style and a content, and we cannot really separate the two. The apocalyptic style uses images and symbols and visions to express religious content. The mysterious "Son of Man" figure of Daniel, Chapter 7, finds an important use in the teaching of Jesus about the end of the world. The separation of sheep and goats symbolizes the last judgement. The Church becomes a woman clothed with the sun and with the moon at her feet.

Apocalyptic differs from prophecy. The messages that

come from our Lady to the world through the young people who see her are truly prophetic. They are prophecies. They do what prophecy does. They call us to reform of life, to conversion. They denounce sin and infidelity to God, and they call us to greater fidelity. They call us to faith, fasting, prayer; they call us to renounce sin and tepidity, to go to confession regularly. They call us to reconciliation with God and with one another. They promise us peace, the peace that God gives.

The messages are prophetic, but many elements that make up the context of those messages are apocalyptic. Prophecy tells us what to do. Apocalyptic tells us what God intends to do. It sees history as completely under the Lordship of Jesus. The future belongs to God. He is Lord of history, in charge of the world and of everything in it. The future lies hidden in the Lord's hands because it belongs to him. He holds the future, and he makes it present to us now in a mysterious and hidden way, through signs and symbols.

Furthermore, apocalyptic confronts evil squarely. Its strong vision of God's power and lordship makes possible a clear vision of evil in this world. Belief in the reality of Satan, in fact, comes from the Old Testament apocalyptic tradition.

In the New Testament, the apocalyptic victory is already present in Jesus. He defeats sin, death, and Satan, triumphing by his cross and resurrection. Jesus overcomes all that oppresses us. We can see that in his public ministry from the exorcisms and the healings that take place.

The ten secrets and the permanent sign

In particular the ten secrets have apocalyptic significance. Two of the young people have received all the secrets: Mirjana and Ivanka.

Mirjana received the tenth secret on Christmas Day 1982. Our Lady no longer appears to her every day. She told Mirjana, "Now you will have to turn to God in faith like everyone else; I will appear to you on your birthday, and when you encounter difficulties in life." Mary has visited

Mirjana every year since then on her birthday, 18 March. Mirjana has the dates for all the secrets; and, according to the instructions our Lady has given her, will tell each secret three days before it occurs to a priest of her own choosing.

Ivanka had her last regular daily apparition on 6 May 1985. Our Lady had been teaching her for some time about future world events, explaining to Ivanka what would happen in the future. This information from Mary to Ivanka is strictly confidential; it has the nature of a secret. Marija, Ivan, Jakov and Ivanka were present for the regular evening apparition. The vision lasted eight minutes for Ivanka, six minutes longer than for the others. During this vision, our Lady entrusted to Ivanka the tenth secret, and completed her teaching about the future of the world. Our Lady asked Ivanka to wait for her alone on the following day.

On 7 May 1985, Ivanka had a vision at her home, lasting approximately one hour. Afterwards she gave a paper to Father Slavko, on which the following was written:

> As on every other day, our Lady came with the greeting, "Praised be Jesus." I responded, "May Jesus and Mary always be praised." I never saw Mary so beautiful as this evening. She was so gentle and beautiful. Today she wore the most beautiful gown I have ever seen in my life. Her gown and also her veil and crown had gold and silver sequins of light. There were two angels with her. They had the same clothes. Our Lady and the angels were so beautiful, I don't have the words to describe it. One can only experience it.
>
> Our Lady asked me what I would wish, and I asked her to see my earthly mother. Then our Lady smiled and nodded her head, and at once my mother appeared. She was smiling. Our Lady said to stand up. I stood up; my mother embraced me and kissed me, and she said: "My child, I am so proud of you." She kissed me and disappeared. After that our Lady said to me: "My dear child, today is our last meeting. Do not be sad, because I will be coming to you on every anniv-

ersary except this year. Dear child, do not think that you have done anything wrong, or that this is the reason I will not be coming to you. No, you did not. With all your heart you have accepted the plans which my Son and I had, and you have done everything. No-one on this earth has had the grace which you and your brothers and sisters have had. Be happy because I am your Mother who loves you with my whole heart. Ivanka, thank you for your response to the call of my Son, and for persevering, and for remaining always with him as long as he asked you.

"Dear child, tell all your friends that my Son and myself are always with them when they ask us and call us. What I have spoken to you these years about the secrets, speak to no-one until I tell you."

After this I asked our Lady if I could kiss her. She nodded her head. I kissed her. I asked her to bless me. She blessed me, smiled, and said, "Go in God's peace!" And she departed slowly with the two angels.

The four young people who, at the time of this writing, still see and speak with our Lady daily - that is, Vicka, Ivan, Marija, and Jakov - each have the first nine secrets but not the tenth. All six say that the secrets have a global significance.

Mary has promised that a permanent sign will appear on a hill near the village, called Podbrdo, where the first apparition took place. Our Lady has told them that the sign will be for unbelievers. "You faithful," she said, "already have signs, and you yourselves must become signs to unbelievers."

Many miracles and healings will follow the appearance of the sign. For believers, however, the blessed Virgin has said that the time before the sign is a time not for waiting but for deeper faith and conversion. "You faithful must not wait for the sign before you are converted. Convert yourselves soon, for this is a time of grace for you. This time is for deepening your faith and your conversion. When the sign comes it will be too later for many."*

---

*This information is from a report by Rev. Tomislav Vlasic, O.F.M., in *Our Lady, Queen of Peace*, a pamphlet published by Peter Batty, Sussex, England, 1984, p. 10.

The ten secrets, and the sign are typically apocalyptic elements. The secrets tell us that God is the Lord of history and of the future. The future belongs to him. He alone knows what the future holds because he alone holds it in his hands. And he reveals it to whom he chooses. The secrets represent the future as hidden in God and completely under his Lordship. The sign, too, is part of the future. We know that there will be a sign, but not what it will be. So the sign, too, stands for the future as held hidden in the Lord's hands.

The mysterious future sign and the ten secrets tell us that we can have hope in the future. They console us because they say to us that we do not know what the future holds but we do know who holds the future: the Lord. And he is with us; rather, we are with him, hoping in him.

True, the future holds some terrible things. But it belongs to the Lord. The terrible things coming do not dim his Lordship or his victory. We can trust in him.

The Light Phenomena and Visions

Father Faricy writes: One afternoon during my last visit to Medjugorje, during the rosary, after I had finished hearing the confessions of some pilgrims outside the church on the side facing the sun, another priest told me to look straight at the sun and I would see it dancing. I tried looking, but it was too bright. He said, "Look again." After five or six seconds, the sun became a flat disk, changed color to silver, then to gold, then to a dull blue. I looked for a few minutes. When I looked away, I had no after-image, and I could see quite clearly.

Many people see the sun spinning, dancing, changing color, at Medjugorje. Sister Lucy has seen the sun spinning many times. On several occasions, large crowds witnessed the sun dancing and sending out rays of multicolored light as at Fatima on 13 October 1917. On 2 August 1981, many say various figures in the sun: the Host, a cross, our Lady, angels with trumpets. And they see other strange phenomena, lights and signs in the sky and on Mount Krizevac and Podbrdo Hill. René

Laurentin has called all these "the phenomena of light." The second evening of the apparitions, 25 June 1981, several people including the pastor at the time, Father Jozo Zovko, saw the word *MIR* (peace) in letters of light in the sky. On 28 October 1981, a large fire appeared to burn on the hill of Podbrdo; police and firemen found no trace of the fire when they investigated. Several times the large cross on Mount Krizevac has appeared as a column of light and has taken the shape of a greek "T", the letter "tau," a symbol of salvation in the Book of Ezekiel, and then been transformed into a luminous figure of our Lady. This phenomenon lasted from fifteen to thirty minutes each time; many people saw it.

Mary has appeared in various ways and at different times to a great many individual persons and to small groups. For example a friend, praying at two o'clock one morning by the side of the church, saw the blessed Virgin pass by her, a glowing figure several feet above the ground.

What do all these signs mean? On 22 October 1981, after a large group of people saw the cross on Mount Krizevac turn into a Greek "tau" of light and then into a figure of a woman, Mary told the young people during her evening apparition, "All these signs are to reinforce your faith until I send the permanent, visible sign." And in August 1982 our Lady appeared to Ivan when he was with some friends on a hillside overlooking the village and said to him, "Now I will give you a sign to strengthen your faith." Ivan then saw two bright beams of light coming from the sky, one shining on the church and the other on the Mount Krizevac cross. Ivan's friends saw the same beams of light.

These phenomena, then, have a purpose: to strengthen our faith, to strengthen the faith of the people of the parish, and of the pilgrims, and of those who read or hear about them. The local authorities, well aware of the authenticating nature of such signs witnessed by so many people on so many occasions, have tried, unsuccessfully, to get people to deny what they have seen. Ivan Ivankovic, a young man of the parish, spent two months in prison because he would not retract his statements that he had seen such signs. During an apparition to the young people she appears to, Mary showed them the head of Ivan Ivankovic while he was in prison. When asked why they saw his head, she answered, "Because he has witnessed to the truth."

All these signs belong to the apocalyptic genre. They give us courage, console us, strengthen our faith. They deepen our conviction that God is Lord, and that his Lordship is one of power.

The prince of darkness

Our Lady makes frequent reference to the devil, to Satan, in her messages. The idea of spiritual warfare between the Lord and the devil is typical of Christian apocalyptic; we find it at length in the New Testament in John's Apocalypse. When we published our first book on Medjugorje, *Our Lady Queen of Peace* (New York and Dublin, 1984), some Croatian biblical scholars objected to our inclusion of a section of an interview with Mirjana in which she speaks of Satan at some length. In the interview, Mirjana says that our Lady told her that our times are greatly under the influence of the devil, that the devil has entered homes and even convents and monasteries. The devil appeared to Mirjana; she describes him in the interview: horrifying, full of dreadfulness. Our Lady came to her afterward to say, "This is a bad time, but it will end." The objecting scholars did not perhaps consider the whole apocalyptic dimension of the events of Medjugorje, and that the devil almost always comes into evidence in that kind of context. He is a classic apocalyptic figure.

In one of the Thursday messages to the parish, our Lady says:

> Dear children, these days Satan tries to thwart all my plans. Pray that his plan may not be fulfilled. I will pray to my Son Jesus to give you the grace that you may, in the times of Satan's temptations, experience the victory of Jesus (12 July 1984).

A month later: "Satan continually tries to thwart my

plans" (11 August 1984). At Christmas time, Mary tells the parish,

> This Christmas Satan wanted in a special way to thwart God's plans. But you, dear children, have recognized him on Christmas Day. God overcame him in all your hearts (27 December 1984).

A few weeks later: "In these days Satan is fighting deviously against this parish ... Persevere in these days of temptation" (17 January 1985). And the next week, our Lady again warns the people of the parish, "Dear children, these days you have tasted the sweetness of God through the renewal in your parish. Satan is working even more violently to take the joy away from each one of you. Through prayer, you can totally disarm him and enjoy happiness" (24 January 1985). A few weeks later Mary asks the parish to "pray, dear children, that God's plan is carried out, and that every work of Satan is turned to the glory of God" (7 February 1985). The messages, then, often show an apocalyptic understanding of reality: the reality of Satan as God's adversary, spiritual combat against Satan through prayer, the assurance of God's victory.

In an interview, Vicka describes what our Lady has taught her and the others about Satan.* Vicka, responding to questions about Satan, says, "Our Lady told her (Marija) that her Son fights for our souls, but that at the same time Satan too tries to carry some of us off for himself. So you have to fight him. He lays traps around us, trying to fool us." Vicka says too that our Lady has taught them that "Satan tries to get in among us who see our Lady and to put us against one another. For him, dissention and hate are everything; in that kind of situation, he takes charge easily. That's what our Lady has taught us many times." The blessed Virgin Mary, Vicka goes on to say, has taught them - and the teaching is for everyone - to take care of their faith by praying and fasting, and then she, our Lady, will be always near.

*The interview is part of a book not so far translated into English. We have the Italian version: *Mille incontri con la Madonna,* by J. Bubalo, tr. S.D. Kozul and G. Amorth, Ed. Messagero, Padova, 1985. The interview is found on pp. 129-130.

"Certainly," Vicka says, "God will win; but Satan will do damage - look at the way people behave!" She finishes the interview on Satan with a typically apocalyptic sentiment: "God is stronger that Satan! The power is God's."

Healings

In the gospels the miraculous healings show that Jesus possesses the Spirit of the last times, the eschatological Spirit, and that Jesus acts in the power of that Holy Spirit. The evil of physical illness is overcome by the life-giving and wholeness-giving power of God present among his people. In the Acts of the Apostles, also, the comforting and healing power of God defeats sickness.

The healings at Medjugorje have the same apocalyptic sign value. They show us that God's power is present among us, active, triumphing over what oppresses us.

Medjugorje has, since the apparitions began in 1981, witnessed numerous healings: spiritual healings and conversions, inner healings and psychological cures and liberations from harmful tendencies such as alcoholism and chain-smoking, and - most dramatically - physical healings. The healings, many of them medically verified, testify God's power and his will to overcome evil in our lives.

9. Ways to Pray

Vicka: I can say even ten rosaries ... but I'm not made for meditation. God hasn't given me that gift.

Marija: I gladly say a rosary, but I prefer to meditate ... I simply must retire into solitude ... I remain in silence.

Ivan: The Bible is the biggest thing in my prayer.

Ivanka: Sometimes I use the Bible, but seldom ... I talk to Jesus in my own words, ... pray with the heart.

Jakov: Prayer is the most precious thing in my whole life ... Every prayer is a conversation with God, ... Heart to heart.

So, as Saint Paul wrote to the people of Corinth: "There are varieties of gifts, but the same Spirit; and there are varieties of service, but the same Lord; and there are varieties of working, but it is the same God who inspires them all in every one" (1 Corinthians 12:4-6). We pray in whatever way the Holy Spirit leads us, because he does lead us: "No one can say 'Jesus is Lord' except by the Holy Spirit" (1 Corinthians 12:3).

There are traditional prayers of the Church which our Lady is recommending anew at Medjugorje. We can pray them in our own way, and if they help us to come to God. Here are some of them, together with some prayers Mary has taught to Jelena Vasilj.

THE FIFTEEN MYSTERIES OF THE ROSARY

"Mysteries" means events to be pondered over. Jesus and Mary remember these events in their lives. We ask them to take us with them, to show us what they remember.

The Joyful Mysteries of the Life of Jesus and Mary

The Annunciation

The Angel Gabriel is sent by God to the Virgin Mary to announce to her that God the Son will be born of her, as one of us (Luke 1:26-38).

Pray once: Our Father who art in heaven,
Hallowed by thy name.
Thy Kingdom come.
Thy will be done,
On earth as it is in heaven.
Give us today our daily bread;
And forgive us our trespasses,
As we forgive those who trespass against us;
And lead us not into temptation,
But deliver us from evil.
(Matthew 11:7)

Pray ten times: Hail Mary, full of grace,
the Lord is with thee.
Blessed art thou among women,
and blessed is the fruit of thy womb, Jesus.
Holy Mary, Mother of God,
pray for us sinners
now, and at the hour of our death.
Amen.

Pray once: Glory be to the Father
and to the Son,
and to the Holy Spirit,
as it was in the beginning,
is now,
and ever shall be
world without end.
Amen.

These prayers are said with each mystery.

The Visitation

Mary, carrying the unborn Jesus in her womb, hurries to help her cousin Elizabeth who, in her old age, is pregnant (with Saint John the Baptizer) (Luke 1:39-55). Mary remembers this time, and Jesus remembers his nine months in her womb. Talk with them.

The Nativity

God the Son is born of Mary, as a baby, in a stable (Luke 2:1-20). Jesus and Mary both remember ...

Jesus is Presented in the Temple
Mary, and Joseph the foster father of Jesus, offer him in the temple as the law orders. But really, God enters his temple in fulfillment of all the scriptures (Luke 2:21-39; Leviticus 12:6-8; Exodus 13:2, 12). "The Lord whom who seek will suddenly come into his temple" (Malachi 3:1). Be there, see it happen.

5. The Finding of the Child Jesus in the Temple
Mary and Joseph lost their twelve-year-old Son for three days. In this mystery we are not thinking of their agony of mind, but of their joy on seeing him again. Jesus explained that he had been doing what his Father, God, wanted him to do. Mary "pondered this in her heart." Ask her to teach us this radical lesson - that what God wishes, overrides everything else in life (Luke 2:40-52).

The Sorrowful Mysteries of the Life of Jesus

1. The Agony in the Garden
God our Father asked his beloved Son Jesus to take on himself our sins - to become sin for us. Jesus sweated blood in his agony to do this, to obey. He remembers now ... "For our sake he made him to be sin who knew no sin, so that in him we might become the righteousness of God" (2 Corinthians 5:21) (Luke 22:39-45). "Jesus offered up loud cries and tears, to him who was able to save him from death" (Hebrews 5:7).

2. Jesus Is Scourged
Jesus, betrayed by his friend, was captured, tried on the word of false witnesses, scourged. He was thinking of us: "By his stripes you have been healed" (1 Peter 2:24). "If one asks him, 'What are these wounds on your back?' he will say, 'The wounds I received in the house of my friends" (Zechariah 13:6).

3. Jesus Is Crowned with Thorns
The Jewish leaders handed Jesus over to the occupying Roman army. They mocked this "king" (John 19:2-4).

Jesus remembers that day. "When he was reviled, he did not revile in return; when he suffered, he did not threaten; but he trusted him who judges justly" (1 Peter 2:23).

4. Jesus Carries His Cross
As a criminal condemned to death, Jesus carries his cross to the place of execution. "Surely he has borne our griefs and carried our sorrows" (Isaiah 53:4). Meet Jesus on that road.

5. Jesus Dies on the Cross
Jesus said, "Greater love than this has no man, that a man lay down his life for his friends ... You are my friends" (John 15:13). "I, when I am lifted up from the earth, will draw all men to myself" (John 12:32)

The Glorious Mysteries of the Life of Jesus and Mary

1. Jesus Rises from the Dead (John 20)
"Christ was raised from the dead by the glory of the Father, (so that) we too might walk in newness of life" (Romans 6:4). "God raised him up, having loosed the pangs of death, because it was not possible for him to be held by it" (Acts 2:24).

2. Jesus Ascends to Heaven (Acts 1:9-11)
"He was lifted up, and a cloud took him out of their sight." "He was taken up into heaven and sat down at the right hand of God" (Mark 16:19). "... and raised us up with him, and made us sit with him in the heavenly places in Christ Jesus" (Ephesians 2:6). "Father, I desire that they also whom thou hast given me, may be with me where I am, to behold my glory" (John 17:24).

3. The Holy Spirit Comes Down on the Apostles (Acts 2)
The Apostles waited in prayer in the upper room, for the promise: "I send the promise of my Father upon you; but stay in the city until you are clothed with power from on high" (Luke 24:49). "And they were all filled with the Holy Spirit" (Acts 2:4). "You shall receive the gift of the Holy Spirit. For the promise is to you and your children"

(Acts 2:38-39). "I will pour out my Spirit on all, ... even upon the menservants and maidservants" (Joel 2:28).

4. The Assumption of the Blessed Virgin Mary into Heaven

Like Jesus, like us, Mary went through death. Then she was taken up body and soul to heaven. We commend our dying moments to her as we contemplate her entry into the glory of God, and join in her joy.

5. Mary Is Crowned Queen of Heaven and Earth.

"And a great portent appeared in heaven, a woman clothed with the sun, with the moon under her feet, and on her head a crown of twelve stars" (Revelation 12:1). "And Mary said ..., 'He who is mighty has done great things for me, holy is his name ... He has lifted up the lowly'" (Luke 1:46-55).

THE FOURTEEN STATIONS OF THE CROSS

"Station" here means a stopping place, places on the road to Calvary where we meet Jesus as he carries his cross. Jesus now risen remembers: he will show us. Look at him, listen, and speak with him at each station.

1. Jesus Is Condemned to Death

"I did not find this man guilty of any of your charges against him" (Luke 23:14) "The righteous man perishes, and no one lays it to heart" (Isaiah 57:1). "Christ died for sins, the righteous for the unrighteous that he might bring us to God" (1 Peter 3:18).

2. Jesus Receives the Cross

"He went out bearing his own cross" (John 12:17). "The Lord has laid on him the iniquity of us all" (Isaiah 53:6). "If any man would come after me, let him deny himself and take up his cross daily and follow me" (Luke 9:23)

3. Jesus Falls

"To the weak I became weak that I might win the weak" (1 Corinthian 9:22). "He took our infirmities and bore our diseases" (Matthew 8:17).

4. Jesus Meets His Mother
"Look and see if there is any sorrow like my sorrow" (Lamentations 1:12). "A sword will pierce through your own soul also" (Luke 2:35).

5. Simon Helps Jesus to Carry the Cross
"They seized Simon of Cyrene who was coming in from the country, and laid on him the cross to carry it behind Jesus" (Luke 23:26). "Rejoice insofar as you share Christ's sufferings, that you may also rejoice and be glad when his glory is revealed" (1 Peter 4:13).

6. Veronica Wipes Jesus' Face
Jesus, "the fairest of the sons of men" (Psalm 45:2), now "had no form or comeliness that we should look at him, and no beauty that we should desire him. He was despised and rejected by men; a man of sorrows and acquainted with grief, and as one from whom men shield their faces" (Isaiah 53:2).

7. Jesus Falls a Second Time
"I am poured out like water, all my bones are out of joint; my heart is like wax, it melts within my breast; my strength is dried up like a potsherd, my tongue cleaves to my jaws; thou dost lay me in the dust of death" (Psalm 22:14)

8. The Women of Jerusalem Mourn for Jesus
"I will pour out on the inhabitants of Jerusalem a spirit of compassion and supplication, so that when they look on him whom they have pierced, they shall mourn for him, as one mourns for an only child, and weep bitterly over him, as one weeps over a first-born" (Zechariah 12:10). But Jesus warns them that if this happens to the innocent, what will it be for the guilty. "Daughters of Jerusalem, weep not for me, but weep for yourselves and for your children ... For if they do this when the wood is green, what will happen when it is dry?" (Luke 23:28-31).

9. Jesus Falls a Third Time
"From the sole of the foot even to the head there is no soundness, but bruises and sores and bleeding wounds"

(Isaiah 1:6). "He was wounded for our transgressions, he was bruised for our iniquities" (Isaiah 42:1-4).

10. Jesus Is Stripped of His Garments
"They parted my garments among them, and for my clothing they cast lots" (John 20:24). "I am a worm and no man; scorned by men, despised by the people. All who see me mock at me, they make mouths at me, they wag their heads" (Psalm 22:6).

11. Jesus Is Nailed to the Cross
"A company of evildoers encircle me; they have pierced my hands and feet; I can count all my bones" (Psalm 22:16-17). "He cancelled the bond that stood against us, ... nailing it to the cross" (Colossians 2:14).

12. Jesus Dies on the Cross
"God did not spare his only Son, but gave him up for us all" (Romans 8:31). "He himself bore our sins in his body on the tree, that we might die to sin and live to righteousness." "He learned obedience through what he suffered" (Hebrews 5:8). "He became obedient unto death; even death on a cross" (Philippians 2:8). "Standing by the cross of Jesus were his mother Mary, and ... Mary, wife of Clopas, and Mary Magdalene" (John 19:25). 19:25).

13. Jesus Is Taken down from the Cross
"Joseph from the Jewish town of Arimathea ... had not consented to their purpose and deed ... He went to Pilate and asked for the body of Jesus. Then he took it down and wrapped it in a linen shroud" (Luke 23:50-53).

14. Jesus Is Laid in the Tomb
"And they made his grave with the wicked and with a rich man in his death, although he had done no violence" (Isaiah 53:9). "My flesh will rest in hope. For thou wilt not abandon my soul to Hades, nor let thy Holy One see corruption. You will make me full of gladness in your presence" (Acts 2:26-28). "You were buried with him in baptism, in which you were also raised with him through faith in the working of God who raised him from the

dead" (Colossians 2:12). "Death is swallowed up in victory. O death, where is thy victory? O death, where is thy sting? ... Thanks be to God who gives us the victory through our Lord Jesus Christ" (1 Corinthians 15:55-57).

THE ROSARY OF JESUS

This prayer, in honor of the thirty-three years of Jesus' life on earth, is traditional in Croatia. Our Lady taught the parish, through Jelena, how to say it properly. It consists of a Creed, thirty-three "Our Father"s and seven "Glory be"s.

I believe in God, the Father almighty,
creator of heaven and earth.
I believe in Jesus Christ, his only Son, our Lord.
He was conceived by the power of the Holy Spirit
and born of the Virgin Mary.
He suffered under Pontius Pilate,
was crucified, died, and was buried.
He descended to the dead.
On the third day he rose again.
He ascended into heaven,
and is seated at the right hand of the Father.
He will come again to judge the living and the dead.
I believe in the Holy Spirit,
the holy catholic Church,
the communion of saints,
the forgiveness of sins,
the resurrection of the body,
and the life everlasting.
Amen.

1. How Jesus was born

a. Reflect on this. (If the rosary is prayed in a group, there can be spontaneous reflection and prayer.)
b. Pause in silence, opening your heart to this mystery.
c. Petition for the grace of this mystery according to the needs of the particular persons for whom you pray.
d. "Our Father" five times (three after the last mystery).
e. "O Jesus, be our strength and protection."
f. Hymn (optional). (Repeat a to f, for each mystery)

2. How Jesus had compassion for the poor, the sick, the sinner, the abandoned, the weary

3. How Jesus was ready, disposed, and open to God

4. How Jesus had great hope in his Father

5. How Jesus was not just ready to, but did in fact, give his life

6. How Jesus conquered and won
Jelena said that Jesus wins when we experience his resurrection within us (interview, Tomislav Vlasic, September 1983).

7. How Jesus ascended to heaven and sent the Holy Spirit
End with seven "Glory be"s and total abandonment to God.

PRAYER OF CONSECRATION TO THE MOST HOLY HEART OF JESUS

Dictated by our Lady to Jelena Vasilj of Medjugorje, 18 November 1983.

O Jesus,
we know that you are gentle,
and that you have given your heart
for all of us.
It was crowned with thorns
and with our sins.
Oh, we know that nowadays you beg us
not to be lost.
Jesus,
remember us when we sin.
Through your most holy heart
give us grace to love each other.
Let hatred disappear from the people.
Show your love.
We all love you,
and wish you to protect us
with your shepherd's heart
from every sin.
Come into every heart, O Jesus.
Knock, knock on our hearts.
Be patient and untiring.

We are still closed because
we have not yet understood your will.
Knock perseveringly.
O good Jesus, make us
open our hearts to you,
at least when we remember
your passion endured for us.
Amen.

PRAYER OF CONSECRATION TO THE IMMACULATE HEART OF MARY

Dictated by our Lady to Jelena Vasilj of Medjugorje, 18 November 1983.

O most pure heart of Mary,
full of goodness,
show your love towards us.
Let the flame of your heart, O Mary,
descend on all people.
We love you immensely.
Impress on our hearts true love
so that we long for you.

O Mary, gentle and humble of heart,
remember us when we sin.
You know that all people sin.
Grant
that through your most pure
and motherly heart,
we may be healed from
every spiritual sickness.

Grant
that we may always experience
the goodness of your motherly heart,
and that through the flame of your heart
we may be converted.
Amen.

HOW TO CONSECRATE OURSELVES TO THE MOTHER OF GOODNESS, OF LOVE AND OF MERCY

Dictated by the Mother of God to Jelena Vasilj of Medjugorge, 19 April 1983.

O my Mother,
Mother of goodness, of love and of mercy,
I love you immensely;
I offer myself to you.
Through your goodness, love
and mercy save me.
I wish to be yours.
I love you immensely,
and I wish you to keep me.
I beg you with all my heart, Mother of goodness,
give me your goodness
that with it I may reach paradise.
I beg you, in your immense love,
to give me the grace
to love everybody
as you loved Jesus Christ.
I beg you also for grace
that I may be full of mercy towards you.
I offer myself completely to you, and I wish
that you would stay with me at every step;
because you are full of grace.
I wish that I may never forget these graces
And if I lose them
I ask you to return them to me.
Amen.

Thank You

Many people have helped us with the book. We want to thank in a special way:

Ivanka, Ivan, Vicka, Marija, and Jakov;

Franciscan Fathers Svetozar Kraljevic, Tomislav Pervan, Slavko Barbaric, Pero, Dobroslav, and Tomislav Vlasic through whom we first came to know the facts of Medjugorje and who has helped us greatly from that time on;

Franciscan Sisters Melania, Ignatia, Amalia, and Josipa Kordic and Janja Boros in particular, for their gracious availability and for all the ways they helped us;

Anita Curtis;

Father Luca Lucic, S.J., for translating the interviews with Vicka, Marija, and Jakov from Croatian and Italian into English;

Father Smiljan-Dragan Kozul, O.F.M., Professor of Canon Law at the "Antonianum" in Rome;

Fathers Helmut Leonard, C.M.F., and Rafael Luevano, for the research they did at Mejugorje, the excellent reports they wrote for us, and their support and friendship;

Jozo and Marica Vasilj and their family, for their great hospitality to us;

Leslie Wearne;

Maria Trefoglie and Father Gabriele Amorth for the useful information passed on to us;

John Hill for his enthusiastic encouragement;

Mark Miravalle, whose doctoral thesis on Medjugorje has helped us and whose example has inspired us;

Sister Mary Rooney, with affection;

Mary, the Mother of Jesus. We thank you, Mary, here now, at the end of this book that we wanted to write for you. Thank you, our Mother, for the graces you have helped us to receive and to have from your Son, Jesus. Thank you for the book, so much more your gift to us than ours to you. Pray for us and for those who read this book, now and at the hour of our death. Amen.

Lucy Rooney, S.N.D.
Robert Faricy, S.J.
25 June 1985, feast of
Our Lady of Peace,
fourth anniversary of
the beginning of the
apparitions at Medjugorje.